By His Grace

Text copyright © 1990, 2001 Hanuman Foundation
Stories copyright © 1990 Sudhir Mukerjee
Photographs copyright © 1971 Rameshwar Das
Copyright © 1990, 2001 Hanuman Foundation
All rights reserved. Printed in the U.S.A.

No part of this publication may be reproduced or transmitted in any form or by any means, electronic or mechanical, including photocopy, recording or any information storage and retrieval system now known or to be invented, without permission in writing from the publisher, except by a reviewer who wishes to quote brief passages in connection with a review written for inclusion in a magazine, newspaper or broadcast.

For information contact:
Hanuman Foundation
P.O. Box 478
Santa Fe, New Mexico
87504

www.hanumanfoundation.com

Revised First Edition

10 09 08 07 06 05 04 03 02 01   10 9 8 7 6 5 4 3 2 1
ISBN 0-9628878-7-0

Photographic contributions: Dada Mukerjee, Balaram Das, Rameshwar Das, Chaitanya, Dr. Kabir, Lakshmi and Parvati

Cover photo: Balaram Das
Typography: Robert Hütwohl, Santa Fe, N.M.

By His Grace
A Devotee's Story

stories about
NEEM KAROLI BABA

by Dada Mukerjee

Hanuman Foundation Santa Fe, New Mexico

Tuma karuna ke sagara
Tuma palana karata
Mein sewaka tuma swami
Kripa karo bharata
Om jaya jagadeesha hare

You are an ocean of compassion
You are the sustainer
I am the servant, you the Lord
Grant me your grace
Hail to the Lord of the Universe

> Verse from "Guru Arti,"
> traditional Hindu devotional prayer.

CONTENTS

Editor's Preface ix

Introduction xi

I   "I Shall Give You A Mantra" 1

II   Winter Camp 17

III   Chamatkari Baba 31

IV   "I Am Always Here" 49

V   Kainchi 67

VI   Hanuman Darshan 83

VII   "Whoever Comes Is Your Guest" 95

VIII "If You Do Not Make It Empty . . ." 109

IX   Abuses, Jokes, and Caresses 125

X   Illness and Healing 139

XI   Last Days 149

XII   Afterward 163

XIII Flowers 167

XIV The Saints and the Sages 171

XV   Epilogue 183

In Memoriam 185

Glossary 187

EDITOR'S PREFACE

This book came into being through a long process that began after Neem Karoli Baba—Maharajji—left his body in 1973. During the next few years, several Western devotees travelled around India, and later the United States, collecting reminiscences from Maharajji's Indian and Western devotees. Many of those stories ultimately appeared in *Miracle of Love*,[1] which was published in 1979.

Many Westerners began arriving in India in the late sixties and early seventies. Some of us were seeking Maharajji, whom we had learned of from Ram Dass in America. If we were lucky, we found him at one of his ashrams, either in Vrindaban, on the plains not far from Delhi, or at Kainchi in the Kumoan hills near Nainital. Sudhir Mukerjee—Dada—was one of the first Indian devotees many of us met. Since he was fluent in English, he often acted as translator. In addition he was a helpful interpreter of Indian culture and manners and adviser on ashram protocol, as well as sympathetic listener to our personal problems and crises. During our time in India he shared his home, his advice, his view of Maharajji's ongoing lila with us. Especially he shared many wonderful stories of his own experiences as a devotee that helped us begin to understand who Maharajji was. After Maharajji's death, some of Dada's stories were collected and included in *Miracle of Love,* but there were so many more. Over the following decade there began a sporadic, and later systematic, taping of his storytelling as many of us returned to India and visited Dada, and when Dada eventually came to America in 1981 and 1985. It was always obvious that the stories were a treasure that should be recorded and shared. In time it occurred to us that they might become a book, and in 1983 the many tapes began to be transcribed toward that goal.

---

[1] Ram Dass, *Miracle of Love* (Hanuman Foundation: Santa Fe, New Mexico, 1979)

The transcribing was painfully slow, as the tapes were not all clearly audible or easily understood. There was a particular desire to retain as much as possible of Dada's inimitable oral style, dear to all our hearts. In 1987 a concerted effort began to actually produce a book, and a draft manuscript that Dada himself had written became the preliminary structure. The enlarged manuscript went through several revisions, with input from Dada himself and other devotees at progressing stages, and with his approval obtained on the final version.

There are many devotees, both Western and Indian, who have contributed to this project, from recording, transcribing, editing, and photographic contributions through generous financial support, loving encouragement and interest. Our names are not important and recognition is not needed. To have helped create this book that brings Maharajji again so vividly before us is reward enough.

Santa Fe, New Mexico
June 1989

INTRODUCTION

It is the soft time of evening. On Dada's porch we listen to the sounds that attend the approaching night: people speaking softly as they pass along the roadway, children's laughter, dogs barking, a baby crying and being comforted; in nearby houses kitchen sounds—of pots being moved, water being poured.

We sit with our cups of sweet tea watching the shadows lengthen, the colors dissolving into darkness. We see each other silhouetted against the last light, and then it is just our disembodied voices that appear to float in a blackness punctuated now and then by the striking of a match or the glow of Dada's cigarette.

The conversation is quiet . . . the silence often conveying more than the words. We are savoring stories about our Guru, Neem Karoli Baba ("Maharajji" or "Baba" as his devotees call him): how he came into each of our lives, how our lives were changed by knowing him, what good samskaras allowed us to be in the presence of such a saint. We compare notes, report incidents in minute detail, struggle to find expression for our feelings about him.

Each new story is an invitation to enter more deeply into the mystery. For to us he represents enlightenment . . . freedom . . . God . . . Rama . . . Hanuman . . . Krishna . . . Shiva . . . the play of form . . . compassion itself . . . a beloved and wise grandfather . . . the closest member of our most intimate family. They say in India that God is like the sandal tree, and the Gurus are like the winds that diffuse the perfume throughout the atmosphere. We are intoxicated.

Each of us knows him in our own unique way. Each thinks that the Maharajji he knows is the true Maharajji. But he is fooling all of us. And seeing his many facets reflected through each other's stories and hearts, we come to know his play; to realize that his identities are infinite. And yet we still thirst to know him; to contain him with our minds. Oh that we could be to him as Hanuman is said to be to Rama: his very breath.

He is our way home! He is the beloved! He is wisdom incarnate! He is grace itself!

In these precious moments there is a suspension of the doubts or disbeliefs born of mind. There is no judgment, only appreciation. The tones of our voices reflect faith, reverence and wonder, delight in being privy to the cosmic joke, discomfiture at our own stupidity, and love so palpable that it is difficult to catch our breath.

There are of course his miracles: his awakening of kundalini in others with a touch, his appearing in two places at the same time, his healing the sick and bringing the dead back to life. But those things are just the beckonings that entice us to the feast. Far dearer for us are the stories of his humanity . . . his sweetness . . . delicacy . . . rascality . . . tenderness . . . his childlike delight in our delight . . . his pain at our pain.

In these timeless moments when we are together, egos are forgotten. We see it is not so important that he looked at us individually or spoke to us personally. For in relation to him we are a single "we." As he speaks to one of us, he speaks to all of us.

For me and other Westerners, these moments of sharing in faith are especially precious because it is so difficult to speak of "Guru" in the West; so hard to express unabashed devotion; so culturally unacceptable to speak of the yearning to surrender to another being.

But now, as we are gathered on Dada's porch with Maharajji in our hearts, it is as if we are not just speaking about Maharajji; he is here with us. Maharajji once said, "When anyone thinks of me, I am with him." And so he is. The moment itself is his darshan.

And as our faith allows, he shows us through his eyes a speck of what he sees: the exquisite web of "maya," the dream that we call "life." He allows us to taste of his peace within, while at the same moment he is buffeting us with the winds of chaos. We are ecstatic; we are confused. And we ask ourselves, rhetorically, "Who can understand the ways of the Guru?"

Dada begins another story. We have all heard it many times before, and yet we know that this time we may hear something new. For who we are at this moment is new to the story, and in this newness is another whisper, another touch of the divine.

Dada is recognized as one of the devotees who has been closest to Maharajji. Their relationship has been so intimate for so long that we treasure Dada's stories about his "Baba" as especially precious. He is our elder brother in Maharajji's spiritual family.

This man we know as Dada also has been Professor Sudhir Mukerjee, a professor of economics at the highly regarded Allahabad University. He edited a prestigious economics journal, was a political activist, delighted in ideological discussions with his many intellectual friends. He was a responsible family man whose household included his wife (Didi), his mother and aunt, and his brother and

nephew. While he had grown up in a religious culture and family, he, unlike the women, had little interest or time for spiritual matters.

And then into his life stepped Maharajji—a barefoot sadhu wearing only a dhoti. He moved right into Dada's home, uninvited. Initially, Dada was kind and courteous, as you might expect, though skeptical as befitting his role as a scholar. But his intellect found itself to be no match for his intuitive heart, through which he came to treasure Maharajji and acknowledge him as nothing short of God in form.

Dada had been offered a ringside seat at the play of the Lord. And the price of admission had been giving up who he had been.

Whatever Dada did, it involved a remarkable degree of surrender. For, by the time I met him, the transformation seemed complete. There was no sign of the Professor; there was only Dada. Maharajji had said to him, "You are mine," and so he is.

As I listen to him speak in the darkness, I think back to when I first became aware of Dada. The circumstances under which we met were so extraordinary that I have remembered them vividly all these years. The meeting occurred in early 1971.

I was sitting on the floor in Dada's home in Allahabad with thirty-three other Westerners. And I was very confused by how we had come to be there. I had returned to India several months previ-

ously and started to search for Maharajji, but he was not always so easy to find. When I had exhausted the obvious possibilities, I decided to enroll in some meditation courses in Bodh Gaya, the place where the Buddha had become enlightened under the bodhi tree.

After almost forty days of practice, I felt the need for a change and decided to accept an invitation to a Shivratri celebration (night to worship Shiva, the Absolute) in New Delhi. A number of other Westerners who had been at the course decided to join me and, boarding a friend's bus, we set out. The route to Delhi took us through Allahabad, a stately old city with wide, tree-lined thoroughfares, and a fine university.

But Allahabad was best known for the Prayag: the confluence of two of India's most sacred rivers—the Ganges and the Jamuna, with a third spiritual river, the Saraswati, coming up to join them from underground. For a Hindu, it is most auspicious for this life and afterlives to bathe where the rivers join, and particularly auspicious at certain moments determined by the position of the stars and planets. At these perfect times, many millions of the holy and pious come to Allahabad for the Mela (a month-long religious gathering where people camp on the banks of the rivers and bathe at the appropriate moments).

When we arrived in Allahabad, one of these auspicious moments had recently passed. A member of our travelling group had been at the Mela and suggested we take a few minutes detour to stop at the place where the rivers meet. It was already late afternoon on our first day out of meditation. We were all tired, and still had some miles to go before arriving at our lodgings for the night. I, as the elder in the group, opted that we not stop, but go on.

But then I began to feel that that decision was not appropriate. After all, we were in India on spiritual pilgrimage from the West, and this spot was among the most sacred in India. A little fatigue should not deter us. I changed my mind and asked the driver to make the detour so we could watch the sun set at the Mela grounds.

When we arrived at that area, it was all but deserted: a vast sandy campground with the river in the distance. The driver asked where he should park the bus. The fellow in our party who had visited the Mela and brought us small medallions of Hanuman suggested that we pull up near the Hanuman temple. Just as the bus was coming to a stop, another member of our party shouted, "There's Maharajji!"

Sure enough, Maharajji was walking with a companion just by the side of the bus. We all piled out and surrounded him, falling at his feet. Most of the group were seeing him for the first time. I was so overwhelmed by this "chance" meeting that I was holding on to his feet and crying uncontrollably.

After some time Maharajji said something and the man with him translated that Maharajji wanted us to follow him in our bus. They got into a bicycle rickshaw and started off down the street. I still could not catch my breath or stop crying and laughing. After having thought about Maharajji for the two years since I first had been with him, the unexpected shock of this meeting left me ecstatic and confused.

The rickshaw led us through a number of small residential streets and finally we stopped at a house into which Maharajji hurriedly entered. As we got down from the bus, the first thing I noticed was the smell of Indian cooking coming from the house. As we came up on the porch, the people greeted us as if we were expected. But how could this be?

It turned out that earlier that morning, Maharajji had instructed the mothers of the house to prepare food for thirty-four people who would be arriving in the late afternoon. How did he know? And wasn't it lucky that I had changed my mind and decided we should make the detour? Perhaps there had been no "luck" involved at all!

And now we were in Dada's house seated on the floor in long rows in the hall and living room. Leaf plates filled with steaming food and cups of hot chai had been set before us. Maharajji sat in the inner courtyard of the house making sure we were all fed what seemed like twice as much food as any of us could possibly eat, but we did. And then came the sweets—mountains of sweets.

It was during this sweet feeding that I finally took notice of Dada. He was a dignified Indian man in his fifties wearing a dhoti, a white shirt, a black vest, and carrying a towel over his shoulder. He was moving through the group barefoot, with a large bucket of jaleebis, a particularly sweet confection which was deep-fried in ghee (clarified butter). With his bare hands, Dada was putting big mounds of the sticky sweet on each person's plate. It was the second time he had come around, so I covered my plate with my hands and said, "Thank you, but I don't think I can eat any more."

My remark and hands didn't seem to deter him a bit. He just said, "You must take . . . you must take . . . Maharajji says you must take. . . " And with that he deftly moved in around my hand and left a big pile of jaleebis on my plate. I was already stuffed to the point of nausea, and the prospect of eating more sweets, which a few minutes ago I would have craved, now seemed intolerable. Yet I realized that in a country where so many people go without food, one cannot leave food on one's plate. So at that moment I looked up at this man with a look which I hoped would convey my anger and irritation: he had just overpowered me. He was looking directly at me and I saw that my look didn't faze him one bit. He was just carrying out Maharajji's orders. It was as simple as that. After all, he knew that Maharajji was compassion itself. If Maharajji said we must have sweets, so we must . . . irrespective of our wishes.

Dada had become so much an instrument of Maharajji that there was no space between the order and its execution. Such a level of surrender was hard to comprehend. It was not as if Dada was a separate being serving Maharajji—he was the service itself. Gone was the decision-making process which chooses from moment to moment to serve, that self-conscious decision-making process that is all too familiar to most of us.

I recall one day watching Dada serve Maharajji. Maharajji was in a very forceful mode—shouting orders in all directions for the maintenance of the temple and the serving of the devotees. From my vantage point on the sidelines I saw that he was giving many of these orders to Dada, and some of them seemed contradictory. After all, Dada was only one person, and yet Maharajji seemed to be asking him to do two things at once. Yet Dada never got the least bit upset, nor did he attempt to explain the contradictions to Maharajji. He would just say, "Yes, Baba," and do whatever it was that Maharajji demanded most recently.

I watched closely. At one point Maharajji yelled, "Dada, go get Binod." Dada was halfway across the temple courtyard on this errand when Maharajji yelled, "Dada, come here." In mid-step, Dada's body turned immediately, responding to the new order which countermanded the earlier one.

Here I saw two things. First, there was no momentary lag when Dada had to process the inconsistency of the orders and decide which to follow. More amazing yet, and something I saw at other times as well, Dada seemed to respond even as Maharajji uttered the first sound of the new order, as if he heard Maharajji's intention before the words were out.

The intimacy between these men reminded me of the one-pointedness of mother-child love, when a mother can recognize her baby's cry from a great distance. I once heard a saying about the tuning of true devotees to their Guru: "They hear his faintest whisper above earth's loudest song; they see his slightest signal across the heads of the throng."

In the late night darkness Didi comes from the kitchen, bringing us yet another cup of tea. It is long past bedtime, but what might sleep hold that could compare with this moment? Our hearts are as one in our love of him.

We always want just one more story from Dada. For his faith never flickers. The purity, the power, and the obvious truth of his stories resonate deep within us, opening our hearts once again to our own innocence, reawakening in us our own perfect faith.

"Dada, tell us again. How did you meet Maharajji?"

Ram Dass

San Anselmo, California
April 1989

I
"I SHALL GIVE YOU A MANTRA"

We are not following the *guru*[1]*;* the guru actually is following us. I say this because I have found it in my own life, my own personal experience, and I have seen it in the case of others, too. *Babaji* came to me himself, unsought, unknown. I had no need, no desire, no idea, but still he forced his *mantra* onto me.

I came from a village in Bengal, which is now part of Bangladesh. We belonged to the landed property class and the income from our property was sufficient for the maintenance of the family, but there wasn't that much coming from it. We had in the India of those days the joint family system: father, mother, grandfather, grandmother, uncle, aunt, children, all living together—a very big family. I was a small boy in that village in 1928, and I had the *sacred thread ceremony.* Just a few months after that my father died.

I had finished my village school education and the question was where I was to go for further study. Had my father been alive, we could have moved to some town or city where he could have earned money for this purpose, but now that was not possible. So I was sent to Allahabad to the home of a maternal uncle—the joint family system providing help and support. I read for exams there and after high school my uncle wanted me to get a job and earn money, rather than continue my education.

My uncle was transferred to another city and went away, but I was able to continue to stay in Allahabad at his house. No financial help was coming from anybody, I knew that very well, but somehow or other I knew that I must continue my studies. I took the only course open to a boy like that, which was to do some private tutoring. Every morning and evening I taught some children in their homes, earning just enough to manage. A number of years passed in this manner.

---

[1] The first appearance of each word found in the Glossary is italicized.

In 1935 I had done my undergraduate examination and had a two and a half month summer vacation. I went to my village near Calcutta, about 600 miles away from Allahabad. On the way, I visited some relations in Calcutta who asked me to stay with them for some

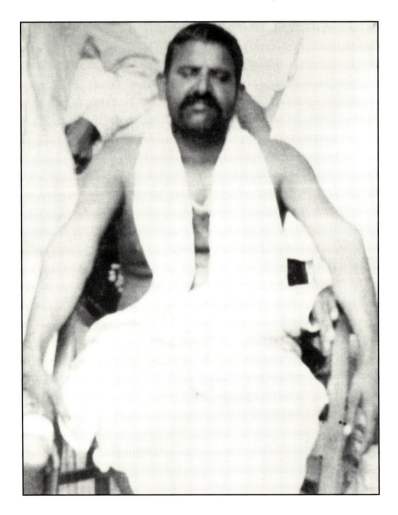

time. While staying there, I would purchase a tram ticket and move about the city for a whole day at a time.

One day I went to *Dakshineshwar*. As I sometimes visited temples, I had been there before. Not that I had any religious interest in temples, but it was a very pleasant place on the bank of the river. It was the month of May, at about two o'clock in the afternoon. It was so very hot that very few visitors were there—a few *sadhus* of the *ashram* were moving here and there. On the bank of the river Ganges there are rows of small *Shiva* temples, not very impressive, just *lingams*. Out of curiosity, I thought I should go and see every one of them. Not that I was interested, but I would be able to say that I had seen them all. When I came out of the fifth or sixth temple, there was a certain gentleman standing there. He was a bulky sort of fellow, with a moustache and a small beard, and a *dhoti* tucked around his waist.

He spoke to me in Hindi, "My son, you are a *brahmin*? I shall give you a mantra."

I said I would not take it.

"No, no, I will give you a mantra."

I said, "I have got no time for that, I do not believe in it." Actually, I was a nonbeliever in the sense that I was not doing any scriptures, any *puja* or prayer, and moreover, politically, I had become sympathetic to communism—reading about socialism and revolution and all those things that were of interest to my young group of friends. However, in India, religion is so much a part of life—the whole family tradition, the culture, the social life. I could call it superstition and be an atheist, but my mother, my grandmother, my nephew, my uncle, my neighbors are all part of the religion. All the celebrations, the entertainments, are in fact pujas, prayers, and dramas celebrating the lives of *Krishna* and *Rama*, so that you come to be affected by it, for good or for bad. As far as my mind or intellect was concerned, I was denying its effect. When this man said I must take a mantra, I said, "No. I have got no time for reciting your mantra."

He said, "When you take your bath and recite the *Gayatri* mantra, you must do it then."

I thought, "This is very strange. How did he know that?" When a brahmin gets his sacred thread, that is the mantra he is given. It is said to be the most sacred mantra for the brahmin. I did recite the Gayatri mantra, not because I understood the meaning or was interested in it, but simply because my father told me a brahmin boy must not forget this mantra. Had my father been living, perhaps I might not have obeyed, but since he died soon afterwards, I did it. So, how did the gentleman know this? It was certainly a very strange thing. In order to get rid of him I said, "All right, tell me." Then he told me the mantra; I heard it. I walked away only a few steps and when I looked back there was nobody there. I began to wonder where he had come from. I knew it was not a dream or my imagination, because I had seen him physically present and I remembered the mantra.

The next day I returned to my village. One day when I was talking to my mother and auntie and grandmother, I told them what had happened in Dakshineshwar. They were very excited, "How lucky you are! You were in such a sacred place, and at such a young age you were given a mantra in Shiva's temple. It is so very difficult to get a guru, even in old age, and here you have gotten a guru. You are very lucky!" That is, of course, what old people think. I said nothing, and the matter ended there.

In the years that followed I completed my university education, did some research work, and was appointed a teacher in the university. After that, my younger brother Subodh, my mother and my auntie came to Allahabad and we were living in a family household. In 1950, Didi[2] and I were married. She was teaching in a government college there.

The month of June 1955 was one of the hottest months you could imagine. One Sunday evening I was sitting and talking with a number of friends in the open courtyard. About nine o'clock at night, Didi, Ma, and Maushi Ma were going somewhere. I asked them, "Where are you going now?" They said that some *baba* had come and was staying in a nearby house and they were going to see him.

Before anybody could reply, one of my friends said, "What kind of baba is he? Does he eat anything? I can feed him." He said it sarcastically. This friend had become a hunter and he used to hunt deer and hare, which is what he was referring to. That shows something about our attitude towards the saints and sages at the time.

Didi and my mother said, "You must not talk like that about a sadhu or saint. You must bear reverence for them in your heart."

---

[2] In Hindi there is a specific form of address for each familial relation, e.g., Didi for elder sister, Dada for elder brother, Maushi Ma for maternal aunt, Chachaji for paternal uncle, etc. Didi became the familiar name for Kamala Mukerjee, Dada's wife. Once the usage has been established, many people of different and no relation may come to use it. Dada and Didi are known by those names by all of Maharajji's Western devotees.

Sudhir Mukerjee next to schoolmate Jawaharlal Nehru, Allahabad University, India.

Sudhir and Kamala Mukerjee in the 1950s, Allahabad.

The women were gone only twenty minutes or so. The house they had gone to was right across the road. We inquired, "What's the matter? Didn't you meet him?"

"We met him." They described the very small bedroom in the mud house where the baba, covered with a bedsheet, was sitting on an ordinary cot. The only light was a flickering candle. When they reached the small porch before that room, they looked at him and he said, "Jao!" [Go!] They had come with some expectation, so they weren't ready to go.

He said it a second time, "Jao!" Even then they would not go. Then the third time he just looked at his hand and said, "Kamala, your husband's Bengali friends have come. Go and serve them tea. I shall come tomorrow morning."

Gone was the light-hearted and loose talk about the sadhus and their way of life. Everyone was wondering how he could know that we were sitting here and waiting for tea. How could he know Didi's name, and how could he know my Bengali friends were here? So it was rather a little mysterious for us. We asked Didi how this meeting had come about. The girl in that house was a student of Didi's in her college. She had mentioned that sometimes a baba came to their house, which we had not known. That day the girl had told Didi that the baba, who was called Neem Karoli Baba, had come. Therefore, the women had gone there. My friends decided to return to their rooms in a distant part of the city and come again the next day.

The next morning I went with Didi to the house. I saw the baba just lying on a cot with a bedsheet on. As soon as Didi and I came, he got up and caught hold of my hand, leaned on my shoulder, and started walking towards our house. He was walking so fast that Didi had to take off her slippers to run after us. Entering our house, he said, "Henceforth I shall be living with you." It was a small house, only two bedrooms, and we were quite a big family.

As soon as he came, he went and sat on a cot. Ma, Maushi Ma and Didi came to the room, prostrated before him and then went to prepare some milk and fruit, so I was alone with him. The first thing he asked me was, "You are a devotee of Shiva?" I said no. He said, "No, no, you go to the temple." Then he said, "You have your mantra also?" I said yes. But I could not correlate in any way that this was the same person that had given me the mantra at the Shiva temple some twenty years earlier.

While we were talking, Ma, Maushi Ma and Didi entered with some food for him—a glass of milk, some fruit cut into pieces and some sweets. He took the milk and a few pieces of the fruit. The rest he asked them to leave there. While they were talking, some visitors began coming. He had been coming to that house across the street for a number of years. We would see many cars and persons coming and going, but we did not know why. There had been no curiosity. I had not heard his name. Now some persons started coming to our house to see him—he was actually a well-known saint in the area.

A certain gentleman came whom I knew very well. When he entered the room, he looked around and, seeing some other persons there, he tried to go out. But before he could do so, Babaji asked him, "You take bribes?" The man began trembling. Babaji said, "Tell me, you take bribes?"

He said, "Baba, in this service everybody takes something." He was trembling in such a way that I thought he was going to fall down, so I caught hold of him and made him sit. He was an excise inspector who had taken bribes and been suspended from his job. He had come to Babaji thinking that he might do something to get his job back, and the funny thing was that the Excise Commissioner, Kehar Singh, the head of the department, was sitting there. And the man next in command to him, Sinha, was also there. I thought what a strange thing this was—here was the confession made before the biggest bosses. The man was given some *prasad* from the plate and asked to go away. After he had gone, Babaji talked with Kehar Singh. Soon afterward the man was reinstated in his job.

While talking with the people in the room, *Maharajji* suddenly got up and told Kehar Singh, "Chalo." [Let's go.] We did not understand anything at all—where he was going, when he would come back, whether he would come back or not. None of those who were with him could help us in this matter; all they said was that nothing could be known about him. We came out of the house. Kehar Singh's car was at the door. While standing there we saw the "hunter" friend coming in a rickshaw. He was only a short distance away when Babaji got into the car. Maushi Ma requested that Babaji not leave yet, but with no effect. The friend missed seeing him by a few minutes and said he would try again in the evening. A short while after this friend had gone, Babaji returned and stayed for the whole day. In the evening when our friend came again, he learned that Babaji had just gone out.

He tried all four days, at different times, but always missed Baba. He tried several times afterwards, but to no avail. His wife and children used to come and have Babaji's *darshan,* but it was not to be for him. He gave up all hope of seeing Babaji. Years later, Maushi Ma said, "Baba, I know my son[3] has done something very unworthy, but he is very unhappy. Be gracious to him and give him darshan."

"All right, Maushi Ma, send for your son." He came that evening and Babaji gave him darshan. This was six years after he made the remark about feeding meat to a sadhu and was rebuked by Ma.

During that first day several persons came and Babaji talked to them. I was only a spectator with nothing in particular to do. But I was curious, how did he know things? In the afternoon three friends came—two were doctors and one was an office employee. Babaji was lying on his cot and when he saw these people coming in he sat up and welcomed the first one—a doctor—and said, "You come in, come in . . . He is a saint." The other doctor was told by Baba, "Go. Why have you come to me? Go and earn your money." The doctor went away annoyed and never came to Babaji again. Babaji took no notice of the third person.

His second visit was after three months and almost the same routine was followed. After his arrival, visitors would begin coming. Often he would go out to his devotees' houses, and sometimes I was asked to accompany him. He would sit for a short while, partake a little of prasad offered to him, and distribute the rest. His talks were mostly about the household problems of the devotees and he would give suitable advice. There was no talk of God or spiritual matters unless somebody would ask for that. People loved him, served him in their humble way, and treated him like one of their own.

His third visit to the house was in December. His devotees began coming to meet him. Seldom would he allow people to sit

---

[3] Maushi Ma had never married, but all elderly Indian ladies call young men "son."

for long. He heard them, gave his advice, and sent them off. This rule did not apply for some of his devotees who would be allowed to stay with him as long as they wanted. Kehar Singh was one of these, an old and trusted devotee, the first one I was to meet. Babaji brought us closer and it was from him that I had my first lessons about love and devotion to Babaji. I met many more friends and teachers afterwards, but Kehar Singh is unique among those who brought me nearer to Baba.

It was during this visit that Babaji talked about our having a home of our own. The house we were living in was neither convenient nor big enough to meet our needs. It belonged to my uncle and we had been living there for more than a decade. But of late we had begun feeling its inadequacy, especially when Babaji came. He said, "You will have to shift from this house soon. Where will you go? Have you thought about that? Your uncle will need the house and will ask you soon to vacate it."

We knew of no talk about being asked to leave. I said, "How can we build a house when we do not even have land?"

"You will get the land."

It was difficult to believe him. It was a great surprise for all of us when the land was actually purchased in a couple of months, after we had given up all hope of getting it in an auction bid.

A couple of months after the land was purchased, Babaji came. "Have you purchased the land?"

"Yes, Baba."

"Now you have the land, so build the house."

I kept quiet. Not only was there no money, but even if the money had fallen from the sky, I didn't know anything about getting mortar, or brick, or stone. After three or four months he came again. "Have you built the house?"

"No, Baba."

He called out, "Kamala, you build the house."

Again, after three or four months, "Have you built your house? Don't do anything. It will be done automatically."

I could not believe this.

While Babaji was talking all the time about building the house, we did not realize how important it was. In spite of all the hardships that we suffered in the house, we were not making any effort or even thinking seriously about building. But soon a relation of my uncle, an old lady of eighty, came to stay with us. It was difficult to accommodate her, not only because of the shortage of space, but due to her temperament. She was always complaining and grumbling. When Babaji came she felt he was getting all the attention and care and she was being neglected.

One day when she was quarreling, Babaji surprised us by coming. It had not even been a month since he had last come and his previous visits had gaps of two or three months between them. It was a busy day full of visitors. The next morning he went out alone and sat by the roadside a few houses away. When I went to him he sent me back, asking me to stay in the house. He remained alone. Visitors were directed to the place where he was sitting. As the old lady saw all kinds of people coming to the house, she began abusing us and Babaji also. There was much unpleasantness before she stopped.

Much later in the day it started drizzling, and Didi and I were helpless spectators. Maharajji suddenly got up, caught hold of my hand and said, "Let's return to the house."

At night when we were alone with him, he asked, "What are you going to do?"

I said, "We shall send her off to my uncle."

"That will not help you. Your uncle will tell you to vacate his house. This is why I was asking you to build your house."

Didi said, "Baba, it is so very difficult for us. We do not have the money. Neither do we have any idea how to get things for making it."

He said, "It will be built and built soon." He left the next day giving us the usual cheer, "Sub thik ho jayega." [All will be well.]

Things began moving fast. Some days after Baba had gone, the old lady was sent back. She made all kinds of charges against us and as a result we got a letter from my uncle asking us to find another house. It came as an unexpected shock. Somehow Baba had a way of knowing things.

At the end of 1957, a friend of mine came one day and said, "Look here, you cannot build your house." He knew our financial condition. "I have talked to an engineer contractor here and the old man has agreed to build your house. You make an initial payment and he will build the house and you can pay him in installments over the years. So try to collect some money."

With difficulty we collected some money and took out loans. That man, Mr. Agarwal, was a retired engineer and a very sympathetic and helpful person. He realized our difficulty and was willing to assist us in every possible way. He and his son came and made plans. Work began within a month.

Ma said, "See how Babaji has been helping you. It is all due to his grace that you are going to get your house." I was thinking more of my friend and the engineer going out of their way in helping us, rather than the unseen hand of Babaji behind the whole episode.

Just a few weeks before the construction of the house started, Baba arrived. Since the old lady had gone away, the atmosphere was peaceful. Ma and Maushi Ma had already become very close to him. For them, Babaji was a very wise and dear member of their household. His talks with them would always be intimate and affectionate. Ma and Maushi Ma and Didi were deeply religious and became close with Baba from the first day he came. He actually began asking about each and every detail of the family and advising them. My mother and auntie would discuss even the minor things of the household with him and he would solve all their problems, family or financial or material. He could be so very affectionate, behaving just like a son to his mother. "Ma, bring me food . . . I am feeling hungry. Kamala, please scratch my back."

Babaji at first called me by my name, Sudhir, or just "Professor." It was in 1961 that one day he started calling me Dada [elder brother]. Others followed, but not my Ma and Maushi Ma. He asked them why they called me by name and not Dada. When they said that a son is not addressed so, he said, "When he is my Dada, he is your Dada also."

One day I was alone with him and he asked me, "Your friends are not coming now. They must be warning you about the danger of coming under the influence of a baba and being close with him. They love you and therefore they warn you for your own good. Am I wrong?" I had no reply to give. He was right.

I was rather an outsider at the beginning, and I was not psychologically or mentally prepared for the difficulties and disturbances his coming created. I was quite interested in social and cultural life, going to the pictures, making friends, addressing various kinds of cultural gatherings, meetings, debates, and I had a very large circle of friends. They would come and gather together just like members of the family. Now when Babaji began coming, there was no place for them to come and sit. Also, many of my friends did not like the idea. "Oh, you have become the victim of some baba!" When his visits continued, they would say I was wasting my time. In spite of all their solicitations, I could not change my new way of living. I was losing my interest in my old life, but I could not think that Babaji had anything to do with it. For me it was just like dry leaves falling from the tree, without anybody's hand behind it.

Maushi Ma had already apprised Babaji about the agreement with the contractor and said it was all done by Baba. "I do nothing. It is God who does everything. Thank God for his grace."

Maharajji with Dada and Dada's nephew Vibuti at 4 Church Lane, Allahabad.

Ma said, "Baba, we do not know God, but we know you. So we are saying that you have done it." Babaji changed the topic of talk.

A few days after he left, the construction of the house started. It was ready within four months and we shifted to it in the middle of July 1958. Some minor finishing work was being done when Babaji arrived four days later. He was accompanied by three old devotees. He showed them around the whole building and explained all about the house and how it was built. "Red house, red house. Very well-built." We had never before seen him behave like an innocent little one displaying his excitement.

One day my auntie said to Babaji, "Baba, you love Dada so much. You have built such a beautiful house for him."

Babaji replied, "Dada's house? This is my house! Dada is my guest."

More than two years passed and there were several visits that he made during that period, but his stay never exceeded three or four days at a time. Whenever he came, someone accompanied him. There were no bags to be carried or any work to be done for him. The only clothes he wore were the dhoti and a blanket, or a white sheet to wrap around his body. That was all he used to have with him whether he was staying with a devotee or travelling. Whenever a devotee would make him change his clothes, he would leave the clothes he had come wearing. His food was also very simple and it was easy for his devotees with modest means to feed him. He was not a burden to his devotees; this we could see from the very beginning. It was much later I realized that, although he was never any burden to his devotees, he himself was carrying so much of their burden.

After that time, Maharajji would come to Allahabad for the winter months, and many devotees would come—Siddhi Didi, her husband Tularam, Jivanti Ma, and many devotees from Nainital, Lucknow, Kanpur and other places. Sometimes Babaji would go out for a few days to Benares or Vrindaban or Jagganath Puri. I couldn't go with him because there were so many people coming to the house and I had to look after them. Very seldom would he take me along. When he wanted to go on a long journey he would ask Didi's brother, who was posted in Kanpur, to send his car and driver, Brijlal, who was an expert driver and also a great devotee.

Much later in 1964, he went to Jagganath Puri with Siddhi Didi and a few others for a week. One day the car came and the driver opened the gate and shouted at me, "Dada, Maharajji took us to Dakshineshwar, to the Shiva temple, and he said, 'I gave mantra to your Dada in this temple.'" Then Siddhi Didi and others who were also there narrated the whole thing in detail to us.

Now all this shows that you do not go to him, he comes to you. This was all his grace, I had done nothing to deserve it. I did not know him. I did not seek mantra from him. He caught hold of me and gave me that. Then he came to that house and said, "Henceforth I shall be staying with you."

II
WINTER CAMP

As I have said before, when I first met Babaji I was not at all interested in sadhus or saints. It was out of sheer grace that he visited our house. Although many unusual things were happening, we failed to realize their importance or to see his hand in them. His visits meant some thrill and excitement and we looked forward to them, but I still looked at him as a kind and affectionate guest. A new process started, however, when we moved onto the larger stage of the new house. Many miracles occurred, acting as shock treatments on me. But no less important was the association with some of his oldest and most trusted devotees, whose love and devotion for Babaji were really my eye opener.

The devotees who started coming to our house when it was built included Siddhi Didi and her husband, Tularam Dada, Hubbaji (Hira Lal Shah), and Umadatt Sukla. They were the earlier ones. We had already met Kehar Singh. Then came Mr. Sang, Inder, Thakur Jaidev Singh, and later Kishan Tewari, Jiban, Ram Narayan Singh, and Gurudat Sharma. When these persons started coming, we were unknown to each other. We were in different stations of life, with different professions and interests, but we were like different streams which come together, reach the ocean and become one.

The devotees would be in our house, not bothered by physical comforts or conveniences, but only interested in being close to Babaji, seeing him and hearing him. This did not mean that we were always trying to hang onto him. He might be in one room and we would be in another, talking about him. Whenever an opportunity came, we would sit together and compare notes—what everyone felt about him or whatever new experience anyone had attained.

After eleven o'clock at night we would be free. We would have finished our food and the whole floor would be covered with beds. Sometimes Maharajji would come out and take his seat on a bed. He would ask, "Are you having tea?" We would say no. "Why are you sitting here with no tea?" Then he would see the blankets on Sukla's bed, and start counting how many were there. "You have got so many layers on your bed!"

Then Sukla would say, with tears in his eyes, "Baba, this is my Didi's house, and she has given them to me."

"Oh, your Didi is very generous to you, she gives you so much. But come and look at my bed and see how hard it is!" This was his way of talking. It used to be the most enjoyable time of the whole day—like the members of a family sitting around the loving and indulgent elder, talking and chatting freely, without any restrictions.

As far as these devotees were concerned, they had been with Babaji a long time and all their doubts, all their questions, had been completely answered. They were convinced and intoxicated. But I would not be intoxicated so soon. I was hearing them talking of Babaji as a saint and as God, but still I could not accept it in my heart of hearts. I would only say, "Yes, of course, it must be so," but I was not believing that. He could not convince and convert me easily. I did not fall headlong like your Kishan Tewari or your Jiban Baba, saying that he is all in all, the divinity incarnate.

In January 1960, the *Ardha Mela* was taking place in Allahabad. The celebration spread over two months. Hundreds of thousands of sadhus came and set up camp in the area of the confluence of the Ganges and Jamuna Rivers. Babaji had arrived in the beginning of December. Some devotees, including Tularam Dada and Siddhi Didi came in December, but many more arrived in January.

One day in January he went out in the afternoon and got into a car, along with Tularam, Sukla, and a few more of us. We did not know where we were going. We crossed the bridge on the Ganges and reached the ashram of Prabhudatt Brahmachari, a celebrated saint. Babaji got down and I followed him; he asked the others to stay in the car.

Seeing Baba, Brahmachari came rushing over. "Baba, you are so kind to me. You have come!" He took Baba around and introduced him to many sadhus. Then he sat Baba down and brought various kinds of prasad from Vrindaban and Mathura and offered them to Babaji, who accepted them. "Baba, the *Ras Lila* party from Vrindaban has come, please do stay the night and enjoy the celebration." Baba readily agreed, but Prabhudattji, who knew Babaji well, said, "Baba, I cannot accept your words so easily." When he had to leave for a few minutes to take care of something, he asked the people in the room not to allow Babaji to go. He warned them, "Be vigilant. He escapes very easily." I did not understand fully what he meant.

Babaji sat talking to the people for some time and then told me that we would go out to urinate. I stood up with him. He told the people he knew where to go. Then he caught hold of my hand and began moving fast. Coming near the gate he asked me to run and get the car started.

When Baba got into it, Prabhudattji noticed and cried out, "He is running away, run after him!" The car started and we drove away.

It was a full moon night and the moonlight was reflected in the Ganges. The motor road was completely empty at the time and we stopped the car, got out and sat there. Babaji was sitting on the road with us around him. He said, "Look at this Ganga, this is not water, but milk. This is pure *amrit* [nectar]." None of us could actually believe that. After all, the saints and sages talk like that, a language we do not understand. The understanding was to come only after six years.

Babaji had a camp at the *Kumbha Mela* in 1966, feeding thousands of people every day. He stayed at our house and in the afternoon, after taking his food, would go to the camp. Many devotees were staying there.

One day in the afternoon, Babaji, Sukla, a sadhu named Omkar Baba, and I went to the mela and came to the bank of the Ganges near the *sangam*. There was a very big barge which was empty except for the boatman's wife, who was preparing food. Babaji got in the boat and I spread the blanket we had brought for him. Sukla had a *lota* and Baba told him to fill it with water and keep it there. We sat for some time until it was getting dark and Babaji said, "Chalo! When you people sit somewhere you forget everything. It is getting late, let us return."

I took up the blanket and Sukla took his lota. We got down from the boat and Maharajji, pointing at the lota, told Sukla to offer us a drink. When we looked in the lota we saw that it was fresh milk! Sukla wanted to bring some of the milk home for Didi and the others, but Maharajji said, "No! Throw it away! You want to bring disgrace to me? Throw it!" Then he had Sukla wash the lota out. I then remembered the 1960 mela when Babaji had said, "This Ganga is not water, it is milk."

On an important bathing day during the 1960 mela, the devotees had gone for their bath in the Ganges, returning late in the day. After the regular sitting in the evening and the meal, everyone retired and slept wherever a bed was available. Some were sleeping on the outer verandah. Siddhi Didi and some other ladies from Nainital went to the roof to sleep. At three o'clock in the morning Tularam started shouting, waking up the whole house, "Babaji has gone away!" I did not understand, but came out of bed and found Tularam and Siddhi Didi standing at the door. They caught hold of my hands and said, "We must go immediately." We ran down the street and found a rickshaw puller sleeping in his cart and got him going.

Siddhi Didi briefly narrated that half an hour ago two rickshaws had come to the gate and a man got down from one and entered the house. After a few minutes she saw three persons leave. It was a full moonlit night, she had seen everything clearly, but it was as if she was in a trance and could not understand what was happening. Only a little while later did she realize who had left.

Reaching the train station, we saw Babaji sitting outside on a bench by himself. He asked why we had come, how had we known that he had left. Tularam said, "Baba, in the future please do not leave the house without informing Dada. It is so very painful for him."

While we were talking, Kanhai Lal and Ram Prakash came back from having their tea. We put Babaji and Ram Prakash on the train. On our way home Kanhai Lal narrated Babaji's escape. Babaji had told him to come in the middle of the night with two rickshaws, and to tell no one. When Kanhai Lal arrived, Ram Prakash was fast asleep. Babaji actually lifted him up and made him stand. We could not understand why there was such secrecy.

Within a few days Babaji returned and stayed for more than a month. One day, after distributing the morning prasad to the devotees, he came to the library room and told me to make a bed on the floor. He said he was not feeling well and would rest; nobody should disturb him. I asked, "Baba, are you really feeling cold? Should I get another blanket?" So I did, although it was already the end of March and quite warm. He had the doors and windows all bolted and then asked Tularam to put locks on the doors from the outside and not to give the keys to anyone.

In the beginning we took it to be another of his *lilas*. The devotees assembled for darshan as usual, but upon hearing the story they all waited outside. By noon the whole verandah and lawn were full, everyone waiting anxiously for him to come out. The ladies from Nainital and some others sat in Babaji's room facing the door to the library and started singing *kirtan*. This continued all day. Everyone was in great suspense. The mood had changed from one of lightheartedness at his usual dalliance to one of deep anxiety. Many persons had tried to peep into the room or put their ears to the door, but with no success.

It was late in the afternoon. Ma, Maushi Ma, Didi and Siddhi Didi were sitting in the courtyard cutting vegetables and discussing the whole thing in a distressed mood. Suddenly someone shouted, "Babaji is running away!" We came and saw that Baba had scaled the wall and was walking fast down the road behind the house.

Many of us followed him. He entered a devotee's house not far away, sat down and began talking as if nothing unusual had happened. To every question he answered, "I don't know." When it was said that the room must have been opened for Baba, Tularam furiously replied that he had kept the keys with him at all times. Someone then went to look at the doors and windows and returned to say they were all still locked.

After some time we all returned with him. Maushi Ma said that before Babaji had jumped the wall she had seen him sitting in the garden near the bushes. He said, "Maushi Ma, I am hiding. You must not tell anybody." After she turned away was when he jumped the wall and was seen.

Later that night when Babaji had retired to his room, we gathered together to discuss the episode. To us, this was the first big miracle. The only conclusion we could arrive at was that this was an indication of Baba's superhuman power. Only his grace had allowed us to see it.

There was an interesting interlude during the 1966 Kumbha Mela. Babaji had a camp and a *bhandara* feeding large numbers of persons every day. Babaji used to visit the camp daily, but stayed in our house at night. One evening there were a large number of devotees waiting for Babaji in the house. As soon as he returned they all surrounded him. I was busy attending to some other things when I heard a lot of noise coming from his room. Someone came and brought me in to witness the fun.

The whole room was packed. Babaji was leaning on his pillow in one of the well-known poses. An old lady was sitting in a corner trying to speak, but Babaji would not allow her to narrate her story. He kept repeating continuously, "Ma, I was dead, I was dead, but I was born in the mountains again." I was very anxious to hear her story.

Later, after she had spent some time with Babaji, she came out and we accosted her. She narrated her story. She belonged to the Farrukhabad district where Babaji was very well-known. Her father had been a great devotee of Babaji, who had visited her father in his home for more than twenty years. When she had last met Babaji at her father's home, she was nine years old. That was sixty-four years ago, and at that time he was already well past middle age. She did not remember ever having seen him wearing a blanket.

She had come to Allahabad for the mela. When her host, a devotee of Babaji, told her that Neem Karoli Baba was here, she could not believe it. She said, "What are you talking about? Neem Karoli Baba must have been dead long back." She had come to verify the statement of her host that Neem Karoli Baba was here. When she saw him, she could not believe her eyes. This is when Babaji said that he was dead and had been born again.

Whenever such a person would come and try to tell stories, Babaji would say, "If you talk about me, I shall go away." But another time a devotee came when Maharajji was in Allahabad. Baba was sitting in the hall and as soon as that person came, Babaji said to him, "You are bringing shame and disgrace to my name. You are exposing me! I shall not come to your house again!" He went on shouting in this way and the poor fellow was feeling very upset. He was a great devotee and had known Baba for a long time. His idea had been that all the old devotees should collect their reminiscences and make a pamphlet of them. He had written to many devotees and they had begun sending some of their stories. Maharajji knew what was going on and so began abusing him.

The devotee started pleading with him, saying, "I will not collect these stories any longer."

Maharajji cried, "Jao! Jao! Go and bring those things you have collected!"

The devotee's home was forty miles away, but he went at once and came back that evening. Maharajji took those papers and said, "Tear them up, tear them up! Go and put them into the fire!" That was Baba's way. He wanted to keep the mystery. He did not want to have beads, or matted hair, or the glimmer of a halo about him.

A friend came one morning and told me that he was having a housewarming ceremony that evening. His revered guru, Sri Deoria Baba, would grace the celebration by his presence. Many disciples, mostly sadhus, would also be coming, and the friend wanted me to

help with the reception. I told him that Babaji would be returning to our house and I could not be away. Baba had left for Benares the day before and was expected back any time in the afternoon. My friend said that if Babaji arrived, someone from the house could come and fetch me. So I had to agree. I went and waited for Deoria Baba. I felt very uneasy, fearing that Babaji would return and I wouldn't be there.

Finally Deoria Baba came with many sadhus and disciples, and when they were seated I slipped away without informing anybody. Within half an hour after I returned, Babaji arrived.

The next morning, Tularam, Siddhi Didi and myself were sitting with Babaji. He asked me if I had met Deoria Baba. When I said I had, he asked, "Did you talk to him?"

"No, I didn't."

"Why? Why didn't you talk to him?" I told him there was a big rush and I could not get my chance. Then he yelled out, "Why did you not take my name? He would have given you darshan immediately!" I kept quiet. But he would not stop without a reply. He began pulling my ear and repeatedly asked, "Why didn't you take my name?"

Then out of my mouth came, "One Baba is enough for me."

Tularam shouted in joy. Babaji patted me on the head and said, "It's all right. It's all right." The matter ended there.

One early morning in 1961, a devotee came and gave us two small pictures of Babaji. He had come from Lucknow and said Sukla had sent them—one for Didi and one for me. Babaji's pictures were precious, but I could not understand why Sukla had said it was necessary to have it always with me. I had neither a purse, nor did I always have a shirt with a pocket. What should I do with it? So Didi took it.

A few months later Sukla came. He told us that he had met Babaji at Lucknow some days before and Babaji had asked, "You sent a picture to Dada to be kept with him? What use has he got for that?"

I told Sukla that I had not seen Babaji since receiving the picture, nor had I talked to anyone about it. All Sukla could say was, "He comes to know on his own. No one has to tell him anything."

Maharajji recited the mantra "Ram Ram" all the time—twenty-four hours a day. Whenever he wanted to write something, he would write "Ram Ram," whether on paper or in a book. If he was to send a letter to someone, he would write "Ram Ram," saying that was his letter. Only once in later years, when I had to apply for a grant for land for the temple at Rishikesh, did he sign his name.

It was in September 1961 that I came to my desk to take out a book that I had been reading the night before. I shrieked and called to the others to come see the miracle. "Ram Ram" was written on the whole cover and a few pages inside. It was all in Babaji's handwriting, which we had come to know by that time. I told them that the night before, when I had left the book, nothing was written on it. Didi said, "What do you mean, last night? Only twenty minutes ago I arranged the table and there was nothing on the book!" Then she took the book from my hand and opened it. Two more pages of "Ram Ram" were there. The ink had not fully dried and we felt that perhaps we had disturbed Baba while he was working. By no stretch of the imagination could we find any clues to this mystery.

I wrote to Tularam about it. Being a close devotee of Babaji and spending so much time in his company, I thought perhaps he had some understanding which I lacked. We had become much attached to each other and whenever we experienced anything new about Baba we used to share it between us. He received my letter when he was with Babaji at Agra, and asked him how it could happen. Babaji's answer was brief. "Dada was remembering me, so I had to go." The mystery was solved.

Some months after that I was reading in my room after eleven o'clock at night. Suddenly the gate opened with a clang and Babaji began shouting and abusing me, "You tease me so much. I was five hundred miles away, but I had to come because you were remembering me. Dada, I always come when you remember me."

When Babaji came at the end of the year for the winter months, Tularam and Siddhi Didi were with him. Babaji did not mention anything about his writing "Ram Ram," but Tularam talked much about it. He said such miracles were very trifling things for a sage like Babaji and that only his grace allowed us to see these things. He would always talk of Babaji as the "greatest sage of the age." His friendship was very valuable in helping me to remove some of the cobwebs that were obstructing the proper working of my mind.

That first "winter camp" of Babaji, as devotees used to call it, was unique in many respects. There were so many miracles that came in quick succession that even his old devotees were taken by surprise. Everyone agreed that never before had they had such an opportunity

"Ram Ram" a page from Maharajji's daily diary.

to spend so much time at his feet and to enjoy his grace for months together. The blissful smile with which he greeted us, his sweet and charming company, the free and intimate atmosphere of the family sitting together could never have been imagined before. This was, of course, before the Kainchi and Vrindaban ashrams were built. But these winter camps continued even after the ashrams came.

The winter camp came to be an annual festival for us—the devotees gathered in a festive mood, free from all worries. I was no longer merely a spectator, but also a participant, sharing everything with the others. And these festivals at home were so entertaining and enjoyable that there was no question of going elsewhere. I lost all contact with old friends and the old social life. The whole process was so smooth and spontaneous that it was only much afterwards that I realized the change.

Yet in spite of the feeling of participation and the enjoyment of his unbounded grace, there was still something missing for me. My mind was full of questions: How are these things happening? What are they leading to? Why does Babaji go on performing these lilas? I could not get into the heart of the matter; everything continued to be a great mystery. There were no such difficulties for many of the full-baked devotees whom I was meeting. They had recognized Baba as something divine and these were his lilas. They had surrendered their doubts and questions, but I was far from it.

III

CHAMATKARI BABA

Babaji's miracles were well-known. Swami Vijayananda, an eminent sadhu writing about Babaji, said that Neem Karoli Baba's very name radiated an aura of mystery and miracles. There were many devotees—not educated or literate—who used to know him only as Chamatkari Baba—the Baba of Miracles. Since we had come to know him, we were experiencing miracles one after another.

One year there was a very heavy flood of the Ganges and the Jamuna Rivers at Allahabad. Floods are a yearly affair during the rainy season, but that year the flood was devastating, even the fort at Allahabad was damaged. There is a *Hanuman mandir* on the bank of the river, and every year the *murti* goes under water. As the water recedes, *Hanumanji* comes out, little by little, covered with mud and debris. The *pujaris* take some days to clean him. But that year the flood was so severe that there was danger that the entire mandir might be washed away.

The pujaris were worried and approached Dr. Katju, the Defense Minister, who was in Allahabad because the flood was threatening the fort. Dr. Katju was a devotee of Babaji and was accompanied that day by another devotee, Bhavanath Bajpi, who narrated this story to me. The pujaris said, "This flood is so severe, many pipul trees that have stood for centuries have been washed away. You must do something to save the Hanuman temple!"

Dr. Katju said, "What can the army do? Only Hanuman can save himself. Of course, Neem Karoli Baba could do it; he is actually Hanuman."

While they were talking Babaji arrived in a jeep, shouting, "What's the matter? What's the matter?" They told of the fears for the temple. Maharajji went to the river and took some water in his palm and sipped it, just sipped it. He said, "It will go, it will go." In three days the water receded and the temple was saved.

In January 1962, Babaji left Allahabad for a few weeks to visit some important centers of pilgrimage: Dwarka, Rameshwaram, Jagannath Puri, and others. Tularam and his family accompanied him. While they were at Dwarka, the head priest of the temple pointed to Babaji, "That baba with the blanket lives here all the time." Babaji kept silent as the priest talked. That was the first time I had heard of him being somewhere else at the same time that we knew Babaji was staying in Allahabad. Afterwards we had many experiences of his being at different places at the same time.

Another example of this happened when devotees had just completed the building of a new Hanuman temple for Maharajji in Panki, near Kanpur. At the time of the official opening ceremony, Maharajji was in Allahabad and told everybody that he wouldn't personally attend the function.

On the morning of the ceremony in Panki, Maharajji went into his room in Allahabad after his bath and said to me, "I shall sleep today, I am not keeping well." He covered himself with his blanket and told me not to allow anyone to come into his room. He was locked in from the outside.

The next day some devotees arrived in Allahabad to give out prasad from the puja in Panki. They described the colorful puja and bhandara and said everything had gone perfectly—Maharajji had even come, although he had said he wouldn't. We said, "That's impossible. Maharajji was here in Allahabad the whole time!"

"Well, he was also in Panki. He was at the temple from seven until twelve o'clock."

After Babaji returned from the pilgrimage to Dwarka in 1962, many devotees arrived and we went on enjoying the *satsang* with Babaji staying in the house almost all the time. One day he went out, accompanied by Tularam, Sukla and a few others. I had to remain in the house. At the time of the midday meal, Ma, Maushi Ma, Didi and myself felt we could not take our food as long as Babaji had not returned.

He was out for the whole day and returned in the evening. The daily visitors had already arrived and were waiting for him in the hall, which was full to capacity. As Babaji entered the gate, he

CHAMATKARI BABA 33

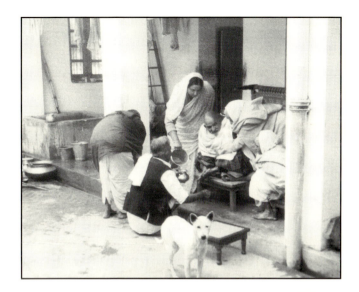

began shouting at me, "You are a fool and have kept everyone hungry. You should not have done that. Bring my food. I am very hungry. Bring it immediately!"

This was very surprising. Usually he took his food in his room, with only the Mothers present. He often said, "Food and prayers should be done in seclusion." But this time he insisted on having his plate brought in and placed before him. He started distributing the *chapatis* from the plate to the people sitting in the room. When one bunch was finished, I took another from the kitchen where Didi was preparing them. When Babaji started distributing the chapatis, there were hardly twenty pieces in the pan from which they were served. When he had finished feeding over one hundred persons, Didi found her pan still full!

After the visitors had gone away, he began talking to me in an entirely different tone. "Dada, you should not have kept others hungry. If you had taken your food they would have joined you. See, Ma, Maushi Ma, and Kamala are hungry. Dada, I was on the bank of the Ganges. It was so nice and peaceful that I could not leave it. You should not keep anyone hungry."

The next day he again left in the morning along with some devotees. Before leaving, he told me that if he were late in returning, I should not keep anyone hungry. If I took my food, others would join me.

After he had been gone only a few hours, someone came and told me that Babaji was on the bank of the Ganges and wanted me to come there. Didi accompanied me. The journey was easy until the riverbed started and it was difficult to go over the sand by rickshaw. We reached the place where Tularam, Siddhi Didi, Sukla and Girish were waiting, but Babaji was not there. They said that after sending the message to us, Babaji had gone towards the sangam, not allowing anybody to accompany him. This had been several hours ago and they felt he must have left the sangam and gone somewhere else. They said it was of no use staying any longer and we should return, especially since obtaining transport was so difficult there.

I did not agree and wanted to wait for his return. I said I would go to the sangam and see if he was there. Girish, a young devotee, accompanied me. The route was along the bank of the river—we could see the Ganges on our left and also the sangam in the far distance ahead. After we had gone some way, Girish looked around and said, "Chachaji [uncle], let us return. Babaji cannot be seen. He must have gone away." I continued going ahead. The same scene was repeated twice more. I didn't want to return, but now I had to think about Girish. He had followed out of his love for me, and if I moved ahead it would be a torture to him, a sad return for his love. But I could not go back as I felt that Babaji couldn't have gone away. He had sent for me; he would give me darshan here. So I was in a fix, unable to move in either direction. Suddenly Girish shouted, "Chachaji, here is Babaji!"

Looking at the river, we saw a small boat coming toward shore, with Babaji sitting on it. The most striking thing was that we had been walking only a few yards away from the water. We had kept our eyes open, searching for him. I was so excited by this sudden appearance that I couldn't say anything. When the boat anchored we got on it. It was very hot out and Babaji had dropped his blanket, sitting in his bare body. Babaji began heckling me with all kinds of questions: when had I gotten his message, had I come alone, how long did I sit with the others, and so on. But I would not reply to his questions, my heart was too full.

There was a *Vaishnava* sadhu sitting with Baba and he began narrating his story. Babaji did his utmost to interrupt, but the sadhu shouted as loudly as he could. The sadhu had come for the *Magh Mela*. The mela was over and many sadhus had gone away. The day before, while the remaining sadhus were in their huts, they saw a person in a blanket loitering around. They asked him where he lived.

"I have no place to live."

"What about your food?"

"I eat if someone feeds me."

One of the sadhus asked if he would like to stay with them. "If you will feed me, I will stay."

After eating, the sadhus prepared some *ganja* and were passing the smoke around. When it was Babaji's turn, he jumped up and began abusing everyone. "These wretched and corrupt drug addicts want to spoil me also. I hate sitting with these scoundrels." He got up and went away.

Some of the sadhus went and searched for him. When they inquired at another camp if anyone had seen a man in a blanket, an old sadhu said, "You did not recognize him? That was Neem Karoli Baba." This was a revelation to them. They had heard much about Baba, but had never met him.

That morning the sadhu had seen Babaji moving before his hut and had followed him. Baba started to talk to him and they had been together all day. The sadhu was jubilant. "I have had the darshan of Bala Gopala [Boy Krishna]!"

Our boat reached the place where the others were waiting. All were happy that we had found Babaji and brought him back. However, it was late in the day and it would be difficult getting back home as no conveyance was available. They were anxious to get back because Babaji had not yet taken his food. Babaji said, "Something will happen." After a few minutes, a devotee arrived in a station wagon. Babaji asked everyone to get into the car and return home, saying he would come afterwards along with me. He insisted they must return as Ma and Maushi Ma were waiting with their food. They left rather reluctantly.

We two were alone. After a few minutes he started asking me questions about the whole affair, beginning with the message he had sent. The questions had to be answered, there was no option because he hammered it out of me. "When you got the message, what did you think about it?"

"I didn't think about it. I just came here."

"When you did not find me here and the people told you Babaji must have gone away and you should all return, what did you do?"

"I waited there for your return."

"Why didn't you believe that I must have gone away?" When I didn't reply he repeated the question. "Tell me what you felt about it."

I told him that my only belief was that since he had sent for me I was sure to have his darshan.

"You thought so. You were right. You had your darshan."

After that I had to narrate the whole episode of going towards the sangam and Girish asking me to return.

"You did not agree with him and continued. But then you stopped suddenly and could not return back or continue forward." I said this was so. "What were you doing when you stopped moving?" For a long while I could not reply. He started stroking my hair and repeated the question, insisting, "Tell me. Tell me."

Then I said, "I was saying 'Ram Ram'." It was as if something extracted the reply out of me.

He whispered slowly, as if pouring the words into my ear, "Ram nam karne se sab pura ho jata." [Everything is accomplished by taking the name of Ram.]

Looking back, I realized how nicely the drama was enacted from beginning to end, finishing with the Mahamantra [Ram Ram]—the crux of all his teachings. The Mahamantra was not for any particular individual or for me alone, but for the generations of devotees who are attracted to him.

While we were sitting there, a devotee brought some food for Babaji, who said he was not hungry. I asked if I could offer the fruits to a sadhu who was living in a nearby hut. When I returned Baba said, "We must return to the house now. Ma and Maushi Ma are waiting for us. We shall take food at home."

It was late afternoon when we reached the house. After the visitors had dispersed and Babaji had returned to his room, we sat together as was our daily routine. The devotees staying in the house were very keen to hear the whole story. Afterwards Sukla exclaimed, with tears in his eyes, "Oh Dada, how fortunate you are. You had the precious mantra on the sacred bank of the Ganges."

A few days after that, Babaji left Allahabad. The day before he left, he told me, "Dada, you stay at home."

I told him I would do so, although I didn't understand what it meant. When I asked Tularam, who was sitting with me, he said, "Udhav[1], we do not understand it now, but we will know in due course." Since then, I have come to stay in the house year-round, except to go to my work at the University or when I was in the company of Babaji or when he sent for me to meet him at Kainchi or Vrindaban. My visits to friends and relations all came to an end.

We never knew when Babaji might come unexpectedly. Aside from the visit during the winter months, he would sometimes come for a short visit any time in the day or night. It would certainly have been very painful if we were not in the house when he arrived.

---

[1] Krishna's friend who brought messages from Krishna to the gopis, here used to refer to Dada as Maharajji's messenger.

In February 1963, Baba said one day that we should go to *Chitrakut*. There were a large number of devotees staying in the house at that time, and when we gathered together late at night, there was much speculation about who was to be included in the party. The next day we took our meals early, and then two cars—a party of thirteen—left for Chitrakut.

It was late in the afternoon when we reached the outskirts of the town bordering the forest area. There were no markets or shops, just a roadside stand where we had our tea. Babaji had me ask the *chai wallah* to prepare our food for the night. Kanhai Lal was asked to search for some accommodations. He said, "There are no houses nearby. How can we get accommodations?"

Babaji pointed to a building a little further away, "That is a government inspection house. Talk to the *chaukidar* there."

Kanhai Lal went, then returned disappointed, saying, "The chaukidar will not allow us to stay without a written order from the authorities."

Babaji said, "You don't know how to tackle such situations. Give him ten rupees and he will open the doors for you." This is what happened and we went there for the night.

After we had fixed up our things, Babaji said we should go and take our food because the area was not safe at night—the forests were infested with wild animals. When we reached the chai shop, Babaji asked for his food, but it wasn't ready. Some vegetables were cooked, but not the one we had specially requested for Babaji. I was much distressed because Babaji was pressing for his food. I rebuked the shopkeeper, who said that since the squash was only for one person and would not take much time to prepare, he had kept it as the last item. It would be ready in a short while. But Babaji wouldn't wait.

He was sitting in the car and I carried his chapati to him, since that was already baked. He knew how very painful it was for me to serve him an incomplete meal and he tried to console me, "Dada, do not be distressed. Get me a pinch of salt. You do not know how sweet it tastes. I have eaten such kind of food very often." I brought some salt and stood beside him, keeping the salt on my palm. He praised the food, "A hot chapati with a pinch of salt is the sweetest food to eat." Of course, I was not convinced and continued to be sulky. Most

of us could not take our food that night as we had already lost the taste for it.

Our visits to different places were to begin early in the morning. At daybreak, Babaji began shouting for us to get ready quickly. We had our tea and were waiting for the *dandi* that had been engaged for Babaji. The dandiwallahs were to come at eight. By nine o'clock there was still no trace of them. Babaji began upbraiding Kanhai Lal who had arranged it. When they did arrive, Kanhai Lal burst out with rebukes at how late they had been.

Their reply was, "You cannot understand how difficult it is to come out in this rain and cold. You have plenty of warm clothes on you, but what do we have?" It was early February and the cold had been intensified by a night of drizzling rain. The two men were lean and shivering with cold. When Kanhai Lal asked them to start they asked for eight *rupees,* although the agreement had been for six rupees. One of them pointed to Babaji and said, "Six rupees for this passenger?"

I do not understand how it came out of my mouth, but I said, "You will have your eight rupees all right, but your passenger is very light." Babaji looked at me significantly and smiled. It still continues to be a mystery how they knew Babaji was the passenger out of the whole bunch of us, as well as my comment that the passenger was light.

We came to Kamodgiri, the sacred hillock. The distance to be circumambulated was a few miles. Babaji got into the dandi and we were on foot. There were a number of temples and places of interest along the way. Babaji would be in the dandi for some time and then would get down and walk. I was with him all the time, either moving with the dandi or walking with him.

As we went along, Baba would be commenting or explaining. We were often waiting for the others to catch up. Finally as we were walking, the dandiwallahs following behind, we came to the place where the cars were parked. I asked whether we had finished our journey and he said this was so. When I looked back, the dandiwallahs were nowhere to be seen. They had simply disappeared! I asked Babaji where they were, as they had not yet been paid. "Dada, they said that they had done a very virtuous act and they would not accept any money in payment."

I got very excited and shouted at him, "Well, they have done a virtuous act all right. But what about their children?"

Seeing how upset I was, Babaji put one hand on my shoulder and began stroking my head with his other hand. The rest of the party reached us then and asked what was happening. Baba said, "Dada is angry with me because the dandiwallahs have gone away without taking payment." Someone said that they must have been paid already. I got furious because only Babaji and I had been with the dandiwallahs and when I was with him money always came out of my pocket. Babaji, all smiles, whispered in my ear, "Dada, do not get angry." So, who those dandiwallahs were I cannot say. It was simply one more mystery.

Later we were standing on the *ghat* before the temple. Across the river a dead body was being carried on a litter by men chanting, "Ram nam satya hai. Ram nam satya hai."[2] Babaji said, "You see, that is how all life ends, with 'Ram nam satya hai.' People take the name of Ram only twice: when they are in very great difficulty, and when they are carrying a dead body to the cremation ground."

---

[2] The name of Ram is infinite truth, traditionally chanted in India by those bearing a dead body to the burning ghat.

After that we visited two other places and then Babaji said it was time to return to Allahabad, although it had been expected that we would stay three days. He said that Dada was angry so we had to return. While getting into the car, he told me, "Dada, one has to return to Chitrakut many times for darshan. It cannot be done in only one visit."

We came to a nearby market town and went to visit the workshop of one of his devotees. The people were delighted to see Babaji and one went to arrange for food while a few others took Babaji around to see the premises. I and two others were sitting with the old manager of the workshop. Talking to us about Babaji and his grace, he recollected an event which had happened years back.

Babaji was in the habit of visiting a nearby village. One evening he came to the house of a devotee where he often took his food. The lady of the house came out crying bitterly and said, "The person who used to serve you your food is lying there." He lay dead, surrounded by the people who had come to arrange for his cremation. Babaji sat down by the man, put a part of his blanket over the man's body, and began talking to the people around him. Everyone was looking at Babaji and listening to him. After some time, Babaji got up and said he would go and take his food somewhere else. No one thought of stopping him. After Baba had gone away, the man lying there sat up as if from sleep and asked, "Why am I lying here?" Everyone was so dazed that no one could reply.

While we were talking, the food was brought and served to all. We all enjoyed the food so much after starving the night before. As we were returning to Allahabad, Babaji said, "We are returning because Ma has prepared *khir* for Babua and is looking at the road waiting for us." Babua was Didi's nephew, a young boy who was in the party. Ma was happy when we returned and said she knew we would be back because Babaji was aware of what was in everyone's mind.

A very striking thing that I had noticed while going around Kamodgiri with Babaji was that "Ram Ram" was written on many leaves of the trees around the hillock. I had drawn his attention to them. All he had said at that time was, "It is like that. There is nothing strange about it." Two days after our return, I was alone with him. He asked how I had felt about our visit to Chitrakut. I asked him how "Ram Ram" came to be seen on the leaves. He talked about the sanctity of the place, how Rama had sanctified the whole place by his presence. Each and every piece of stone bears his footprints on them. Even the plants and trees, because of their association with him, treasure his name in their bosom. Babaji said, "'Kan kan me Rama hai' [Rama is present in each and every particle], and his devotees get his darshan even now."

That night in Allahabad when we had just returned from Chitrakut, Babaji was in his room and the Mothers were with him. Maushi Ma said, "Baba, you are very kind to everyone, but not to these old women."

"Why, Maushi Ma?"

"You took everyone to Chitrakut, but left us behind."

"Maushi Ma, Chitrakut is a rocky area and it is very difficult for you to visit such a place. We shall go to Vindhyachala and you will have the darshan of the *Vindhyavasini Devi*. We shall go tomorrow."

The next day a large party started early in two cars. Didi and her sister Ashoka stayed behind to look after the household duties. After visiting the temples we were returning and Babaji said he would go to urinate. Babaji told the others to remain in the car, and I walked with him some distance into a field. After urinating, we had walked back a bit when he suddenly sat down and said a thorn was stuck in his foot. I also sat down, not in front of him as I normally would, but behind him. Everyone in the car came rushing out and some began examining his foot. Mr. Joshi took a pin from the turban on his head and began searching for the thorn. I was sitting behind Babaji, supporting his head which he had placed on my shoulder. Little by little he leaned his whole body on me. It was so light. Suddenly it

came to me in a flash what I had said the day before to the dandiwallahs in Chitrakut, that their passenger was very light. I felt that this communication had been his, with my mouth serving as his instrument. This happened many times afterwards also.

A month after Babaji left Allahabad, Didi's father died and we had to go to Kanpur to attend the ceremony. We had had no news of Babaji since he had left, but somehow I had the feeling that we would meet him there. When we reached Kanpur, Didi's sister Ashoka and her uncle were waiting for us at the station, saying they had just received word that Babaji had arrived and was staying with Dr. Diksit. We went to his house, but Babaji was not there, having gone to a devotee in another part of the city. This house was situated some distance from the main road and was reached by going through a narrow lane. We got down from the car and had started down the dark lane when an old devotee came carrying a flashlight. He had been sent by Babaji, who told him that we were coming and should be met at the road with a lamp.

Babaji was sitting on the open roof surrounded by a number of devotees. There was much jubilation in our meeting. I offered Babaji a packet of sweets I had brought for him from Allahabad. He exclaimed, "How did you know that I would be here?" I did not reply. After some time he asked me to go home and take my bath, as was my custom, and he would come and visit us there. As I was leaving, he wanted to give me some prasad but there was nothing nearby. He took off the garland that was around his neck and offered that to me, saying, "You have given me so much, but what shall I give you? These people are *badmash*. They do not keep anything for me. You take this from me." I was overwhelmed by his grace, the soft and affectionate words, and the sacred prasad offered to me.

He visited us that night and spent some time with Didi's brother and his family. Next morning he sent for me, knowing there was no work for me to do in that house. I spent the whole day with him. In the evening when he was leaving Kanpur, he dropped me near Mr. Choudhury's (Didi's brother's) house and I returned to Allahabad that night.

It was all a unique lesson for me. When we had to go to Kanpur I was distressed with the idea. It was only a year back that Baba had asked me to stay at home. Here, at the first opportunity, I was disobeying him and I was not happy about it. Had it not been so important for us to attend the function, I would not have left the house. Faced with this situation, I suddenly felt that I would meet him there and that he wanted me to go. This was the first time I felt this method of communication. Afterwards I became more accustomed to it.

Even now, since he has left his body, it goes on. A few years ago, when the Western devotees were asking me to come to America, I could not take it seriously. It seemed too great a burden to put on those persons. But pressure continued on every side, and for days and months I was feeling very helpless about it. Then late one night I was reading in my room after everyone else had gone to sleep. The door to Babaji's room was open and I went and bowed at his bed. Suddenly I felt that he said, "You should go." The next day I wrote them saying that I would come.

CHAMATKARI BABA

IV
"I AM ALWAYS HERE"

My mother and aunt were deeply religious and accepted Babaji as the head of the family. Ma would often tell us that the family and the household belonged to Baba and we were all his children. Her whole treatment of him was based on the fact that Babaji knew what was in the minds of everyone and behaved accordingly. He treated them as his Ma and Maushi Ma, giving them all the freedom and indulgence and grace. They reported to him everything going on in the house and sought his advice and guidance for running it. The most important duty assigned to them was to prepare the food and feed everyone coming to him. "Ma khana khilao" [Ma, make food] was his pet method of asking them to feed the people. Often emphasizing the importance of their work, he would say, "Maushi Ma, this is the home of the deity. Here everyone gets his food, so I also get mine."

My mother was from a very orthodox brahmin family and formerly she could not imagine that a lower caste person would enter the kitchen. None of the servants were allowed to dust or sweep there or bring in the drinking water from outside. Ma was like that and I could not have thought of changing her attitude. But with Maharajji around all those things eventually changed. Westerners came and were entering the kitchen. Ma also became reconciled to Muslims entering the house. Maharajji was not forcing her to do this; her whole outlook had changed. She began feeling that all were her sons and daughters. If she is not keeping me away from her kitchen, how could she go on keeping others away? Now, from where had this wider outlook come? Of course, Maharajji had done that, but all he had said was, "Ma, give food to all."

Ma and Maushi Ma had become accustomed to treating Babaji as their near and dear one, and would talk to him without any formality. Babaji enjoyed that. Whenever he left for any place, they would invariably ask him where he was going, when he would come again, and sometimes they asked him to extend his stay in the house.

Maharajji with Dada's mother and aunt, Ma and Maushi Ma.

Maharajji with Dada, Ma and Maushi Ma.

Once Babaji came and left two days later. Ma asked him to stay for a few days more. He said, "Ma, let me go now. I have some important work to attend to. I shall return soon."

Ma said, "You have no work as such—the only work that you have is to run away."

He laughed and said again that he would return soon. Three months passed and he had not come back. Ma said, "Look, so much time has passed. This is low. He goes on bluffing us." Babaji arrived a few days later. When they came to see him in his room, the first thing they said was, "Baba, you speak so many lies. You promised you would return soon. Now you have come after three months!"

Babaji replied in his inimitable way, "Ma, where do I go? I am always here. Believe me, Ma, I never speak lies to you. I am always here."

He could be so very affectionate, behaving just like a son to the Mothers. His great power, the miracles and such, no doubt were there, but the very soft, delicate, sweet and innocent impressions left by him provided a perennial source of joy—that human aspect.

At night in Allahabad, Baba would take his food in his small room and the Mothers would sit with him. Didi would be busy preparing the chapatis and my duty was to carry them one by one to him. After he finished his food he would go on talking to those Mothers in a very relaxed mood. Sometimes he would take two spoons and begin to play on the head of one of the Mothers. Once Didi made some curd and gave quite a large tumbler of it to Babaji. He took a whole spoonful and put it on the head of one of the Mothers. Fortunately, her *sari* was over her head. Such kinds of things would go on.

One time when Babaji was at our house, he went for his toilet and gave me his blanket, "Here, you hold it." I put it on the cot and was standing near him because he was talking. He began abusing me, "What have you done with my blanket? You have left it there. Look what they are doing!"

I turned and saw that Didi, my mother, my auntie, and Siddhi Didi had picked up that blanket and were actually smelling it. When I came to them they said, "Look here. It has the odor that comes from the body of a newborn child."

Babaji shouted, "Where is my blanket!"

One day in the house, Baba stopped before a picture of himself as a younger man. "Whose photo is this?" he said. Since it was a photo of himself, of course, I did not reply. Then he whispered, "How did you recognize?" I suddenly realized that this photo was of Maharajji as I had first seen him so many years ago in Dakshineshwar.

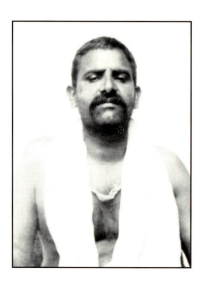

One day when Maharajji was not in Allahabad, my mother prepared khir, a delicacy that is often offered to the gods or goddesses. My mother put it in a big bowl and said, "If Babaji comes today, it will be very good. I will have this khir to serve him." Of course, she was not really expecting him.

Much later in the day after we had taken our food, Babaji suddenly came. "You have prepared khir? I have come for it." Ma was so happy to see him eating it. When he was finished, he said, as if suddenly remembering, "Oh, what a mistake I have made! Today is ekadasi [a day of fasting], and here I am eating khir!" Now this was Babaji's way, the sweetness that we remember.

From the beginning of my being with him, he would often need to wipe his mouth. I would have a handkerchief, but if that was soiled I would just offer him my dhoti. He knew that some people thought that this was a sacrilege. One day Babaji created a drama. After drinking a glass of milk, a little remained clinging to his moustache.

He grabbed at my dhoti and rubbed it on his moustache, saying, "You are interested in something else and not paying attention to me!"

When Baba was in our house, we would purchase sweets or other devotees would bring them to be distributed as prasad. Baba would often give them to me to distribute to all the family. My mother said, "It is very strange. You make us eat, but you do not eat. Why?"

"Babaji does not give me to eat, he gives me to distribute."

Later Ma and Maushi Ma said to Baba, "Dada says that you give him sweets to distribute, but not to eat."

Baba said, "What necessity has he for eating sweets?"

I didn't understand the meaning of that at the time. Much afterwards I came to understand that prasad is something that has been consecrated and its purity must be kept. If you put it into your mouth, it becomes jutha [impure]. But impurity can come not merely by touching it with your tongue, but also by touching with your mind. If your desires, your greed, are concentrated on it, it also becomes impure. Is it not that? It is said in the scriptures that when you offer something to God, He does not come with an open mouth, but takes it just by his glance. I felt that Babaji also accepted offerings just by his glance and saying "Thik hai." [All right.] If I was distributing with the thought that

I also shall eat, it would become impure. It would become not Baba's prasad, but the refuse from Dada's plate, a great sacrilege. So in order to make me immune from that, he took away the taste from my tongue and the desire from my heart.

One day, Mr. Mathur, a devotee from Benares, and I were sitting on the porch, sipping our tea and talking. Suddenly the gate was opened and a very frightened dog ran in and went around the back of the house.

This dog: about a year earlier, we had heard a dog shrieking outside in pain. It had been beaten so mercilessly that the skin was off. I took a bottle of lotion and powder and put it on the bloody wound. After a few days the wound healed, but the dog would not leave the street, so we began feeding it. She became so attached that she stayed close by, but would not come inside the house. This was the same dog that had just run in the gate.

About a dozen young men with sticks in their hands came and said, "Where is your dog?"

I said, "My dog?"

"Yes, your dog. She just entered into your compound."

"What's the matter?"

"We shall kill her. She has eaten three of our chicks."

I said, "She is not my dog, neither could she have eaten your chicks."

They insisted they would find and kill her. "You know how much it costs? It costs three rupees for a chick."

"She has eaten three?" I took out a ten rupee note from my pocket and gave it to them. They wanted to return one rupee, but I said, "Keep that to have your tea. Just go."

Later that day we received a telegram from Babaji saying that he would be travelling on a train which would be passing through Allahabad. In a short while, Kanti (Siddhi Didi's daughter-in-law) and Didi had both prepared Babaji's food to be taken to the station. They thought that Babaji was going to Delhi. Somehow the idea came and I said, "Look here, Kanti, if you and your chachiji [auntie] go with *tiffins,* Babaji will certainly think that you do not want him to stop here. Let Ramesh (Siddhi Didi's son) and myself go there. After all, we are uncle and nephew, and

we may be able to muster sufficient strength to get him down. If you two people come with his food, he is sure to think you have come to see him off."

Ramesh and I reached the station and found the train had already arrived. We found Babaji in a compartment. "You got my telegram?"

"Yes."

"So what happened?" He kept asking questions. "And what happened after that?" Ramesh told him of Kanti and Didi preparing food. "Then what happened? Then what happened?"

"Then Chachaji [uncle] said to them not to come. He said, 'If you bring food, that means that you think Babaji will continue his journey and you have come to see him off. Let Ramesh and myself go. . .'" Then Ramesh got to the part about "Uncle and nephew might have the strength between them to get him down."

Baba said, "Yes, yes, of course, uncle and nephew have got plenty of strength. I shall get down."

As we were getting off the train, Jiban, who had been travelling with Maharajji, came running. He had been searching for us along the platform. We took two rickshaws—Jiban and Ramesh in one, Babaji and I in the other. Babaji began talking, "You have done a very big thing." I didn't understand what he was saying; I kept quiet. "The dog was neither yours, nor had she eaten the chickens. But in order to save her life, you gave that money."

One day Baba and I went out toward the bazaar and Babaji sat down by the roadside. It was a poor area of the town and people and animals were crowding around. He said, "Dada, I am feeling very hungry. I would like to have a chapati and some water."

I could not leave him and return to the house, it was quite a few furlongs away. I said, "Shall we go home?"

"No, no, Dada, if we go home now they will serve me a great meal. Just get something from here. Go ask at some house."

I went to a nearby house, feeling a little shy about asking for food as they were all poor people there. To my surprise, I found at that house a young man who was a student in the university. He also was surprised to see me. "Sir, how are you here?"

I said, "Battacharya, you have got to give me a chapati and some water."

"Oh, why only one chapati? I shall get some food also." I said no, and took just two chapatis from him and a tumbler of water.

Babaji ate the chapatis and said, "Bas. Thik hogaya. [Enough. Fine.] I was very hungry. Rukha sukha khao, thanda pani piyo." [Eat unbuttered, dry bread and drink cold water and you are fully satisfied.] When we returned, he told Ma and Maushi Ma, "I have eaten very well."

The whole story was narrated and then someone said, "Well, Dada, do you know what he has done with you? This is one of the highest duties of the disciple—to beg food for his guru. He has made you do it."

One winter, while Babaji was away, Ashoka came from Delhi accompanied by a lady not known to us. This woman began behaving as if she were an old relation returning home after a long lapse of time. She addressed Didi as Mataji [mother] and called me Pitaji [father], and Ma and Auntie as Dadiji [paternal grandmother]. She was completely free and unconventional in her behavior, like taking clothes from Didi's wardrobe and distributing them to others. She spoke of her high-placed relations, including the governor of a state. After waiting several days for Babaji, she decided to go in search of him. "Pitaji, I am not fortunate enough like you to have his darshan sitting at home. I have to go in search of him." She took the addresses of some devotees at Lucknow, Bareilly and Nainital where he might be found.

Ashoka told us how she had met the lady, named Neela Devi, in the course of her journey. They had been travelling in the same compartment of the train. When asked where she was going, Ashoka said she was headed to her sister's house in Allahabad to meet Neem Karoli Baba. Hearing Babaji's name, this unknown lady blurted out that she would accompany Ashoka because she had been searching a long time to meet Baba again.

A week later Babaji came and Neela Devi was with him. After two days, Baba sent her away. She left Babaji two very valuable things; a silver statue of Shirdi Sai Baba, and a beautiful silver Shiva lingam with *Narmadeshwar* in it. He offered them to Ma and Maushi Ma, asking that they put them in the puja room and perform their puja as they did with other deities.

After Neela Devi had gone, there came many complaints from the devotees she had visited at Lucknow and Nainital. Even in Allahabad, Didi and others were not happy with the way she had thrown away so many things. When Babaji returned a few months later, he began talking about the hue and cry raised against her. She had been accommodated because she took his name. Babaji said he had no hand in it; he had not instigated her to do so. Babaji was narrating this before many devotees sitting around him, often raising his voice and abusing someone, showing he was seriously concerned with the matter.

Suddenly he declared that it was I who was responsible for it. If I had not allowed her to enter the house and given her the addresses, all this mischief would not have taken place. My reply was, "What else could I have done? You sent her and my task was to receive her."

He yelled at me, "I sent her? You say I sent her!"

With some excitement I said, "How could anybody come to this house without your knowledge? You knew her."

He said, "So many of Kamala's things are gone."

"They must have been useless things. Had they been valuable, they would not have gone."

He seemed to cool down and said in a dejected tone, "If Dada talks like that to me, what can I do?" It was a perfect act and the mystery remained.

Several months after that, when I was alone with him, he told me almost in a whisper, "Dada, Neela Devi has given 18,000 rupees for a temple."

She had said one day when she was with us, "Pitaji, you must have a temple of Hanumanji in Babaji's name. Your daughter has the money for that."

Many years later a certain lady entered the gate and shouted, "Pitaji, you do not recognize your daughter?" It was Neela Devi. She had been involved in some family strife regarding her share of ancestral property. After much litigation, she had acquired it. She told us that Babaji had forbidden her to visit or correspond with us until this work was completed.

When Maharajji had drawn anyone to him, he cared for and protected that person. He would provide whatever was needed. Whether you took it or not, that was up to you. Occasionally, however, he did force.

One winter, a relation of Dharm Narayan Sharma came to Allahabad to see Babaji. That evening this man was to go to Calcutta for a job interview with the railway board. He was seeking Maharajji's *ashirbad* so that he would be successful. When he was to leave, Babaji said, "Don't go."

The man said, "No, Baba, I must go."

But Babaji was insistent. They argued, but ultimately the man had to give it up. He said to me, "Dada, I came to him for his ashirbad, so I could get that job. Now he has stopped me." He was very bitter.

The next morning the man ran into the house, shouting, "Dada, see how Babaji has saved my life!" The newspaper had come and he learned that there had been a very serious accident at the Mogul Serai railway station. Two trains had collided and about two hundred persons had died. One of the bogies that was smashed was the bogie in which he would have been travelling.

A young Englishman named Lawrie once stayed in Babaji's ashram at Hanumanghar for about a year. He had been interested in

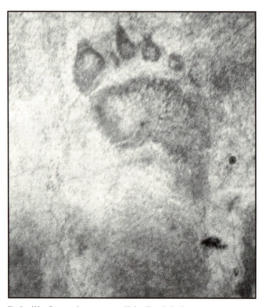

Babaji's footprints on wall in Dada's house.

India's spiritual heritage and had come to India to learn about it. He had met Babaji, secured his grace, and was allowed to stay in the ashram, studying with Haridas Baba.

One day some devotees were talking to Babaji about Lawrie and his spiritual practice. Babaji said he would soon be going away—his *"maya"* was coming and would take him back to England. Some days later, Lawrie's lady friend, Susan, arrived in Nainital. Babaji told Didi that they would be visiting Allahabad and would stay in the house for some days and she should arrange for them.

Didi arranged a small room for their use. When she had opened the door to fix up the room, she found that one wall was full of footprints. She was astonished to see them and was convinced that they were Babaji's. Many devotees came to see the footprints and believed them to be Babaji's, but could not understand what they indicated.

A few days later, Lawrie and Susan arrived. Every attempt was made to make their stay comfortable, but there were some difficulties about their food. Lawrie was used to pure vegetarian cooking, but Susan was not. She complained to Didi directly that she was losing her health because her food was being neglected. This was hard for Didi, who had taken so much care with all the arrangements. Tears came in her eyes.

Shortly after, a devotee came with his car. He had received a phone call from Baba, asking him to take Lawrie and Susan to his house for a few days. They had been "transferred."

Babaji arrived after a few days and consoled Didi. He explained that Lawrie and Susan were old friends who were planning to marry. When Lawrie did not return from India, Susan came to bring him back. They had no money and didn't know what to do.

They were given the passage money. On the day they were to leave, Babaji left for Chitrakut with some devotees. He told me to accompany Lawrie and Susan to the station that afternoon. With tears in his eyes, Lawrie begged to be excused for all their lapses.

The devotee in whose house they had been staying also came to the station and then gave me a ride home in his car. We sat on the porch and he told me about the strange behavior of his guests. They had stayed in their room all the time, bolting it from inside. This created some suspicion in his mind. It was the time of the Indo-Chinese conflict and he thought they were spies, transmitting radio messages from the closed room. When he made that statement, I could not listen to him any longer. He had his tea and prasad and then left.

Soon after, another car pulled up with Babaji in it. He sent the people who had come along with him into the house, and he came and sat with me. He asked about the whole episode. "You went by rickshaw to the station? Did Didi accompany you? They went in the car? What did Lawrie say?" All these things he recounted to me, rather than asking. "How did you return? You came by car? It was good of him to bring you home. You must have offered him tea and prasad." These were all preliminaries. "You were talking? What was he saying about them? Why did he go away so early? Weren't you talking to him?"

After repeated inquiries, I had to disclose that man's suspicion about Lawrie and Susan being spies. "You became angry with him because you did not believe that? Why didn't you believe him? Why?"

After that kind of hammering I said I was annoyed because I could not imagine how a person who claimed to be a devotee could think that Babaji would put him in such a dangerous situation. I said to Baba, "You knew everything about them and you could not do anything that would create trouble."

He was stroking my head while I was talking. When I stopped he laughed and said, "Do you think that everyone is a fool like you? There are wise people who look at things differently."

Once Maharajji had gone from Allahabad to Jagganath Puri with some of the devotees. I could not go because I had to run the household. At about four o'clock one afternoon I was relaxing, my mother and auntie were resting in their room, when I heard some noise from behind the house. Some children were shouting, "Baba, Baba, let us have the flute!"

A man's voice came, saying, "I am hungry, give me some food."

I looked out and saw that many children were surrounding a tall fellow with long hair, wearing a long coat. He had a brass flute in his hand. Seeing me, he said, "I am hungry."

He came and sat just before the door and I went to get some chapatis and *dal*. I brought them and said, "These are not fresh, they were cooked at noon, but eat them and after that you can have some sweets."

He would not lift his head, just looked down and said, "Araharki dal, araharki dal. I have not eaten araharki dal for so many years."

I remembered that Maharajji had brought some sweets from Vrindaban, saying, "This is Biharaji [Krishna] prasad." I brought some to the man. When he had finished and was getting up, I said, "Wash your mouth, wash your mouth," as there was dal on his beard. But he would not, and when I insisted he only washed his flute. When he was leaving I said, "Baba, you can come whenever you like. If I am not at home, my mother and auntie will welcome you."

He said, "I have been searching long for the house where bhakti [devotion] and *Lakshmi* live."

During all this, Ashoka had been standing nearby. Just like a statue. Later she related that while recently in Delhi, she and a friend had gone out in a car with Maharajji. They had stopped at the house of a very wealthy man and Maharajji had gone inside, telling them to wait at the gate. While they were waiting, a man came who looked exactly like this man, except instead of a flute he carried a big stick. He said he was very hungry and asked for food, but the gatekeeper would not let him in. He said, "I have come to the house of the richest man in the city and I must return disappointed."

Two days after that, Maharajji returned. He said to me, "Biharaji gave you darshan." When the story was narrated, Jivanti Ma asked me, "Dada, on what day did that person come who ate the araharki dal?" I said it was Thursday. Then she said, "We were in Jagganath Puri then and Maharajji had already taken his food. Suddenly at about four o'clock he said, 'I shall eat chapati and araharki dal.' He does not eat araharki dal, you know that, he always eats mung dal. So we were rather surprised. Didi said, 'This is not the time for your food, you have eaten already. Besides, you do not eat araharki dal.' But Babaji kept saying, 'I am hungry and you do not give me food.' So we had to go and get araharki dal to cook for him. That was the same time you were feeding araharki dal to that man with the flute in Allahabad."

When Babaji started spending a few months at Allahabad, the news spread among his devotees living in different parts of the country. Many of them came to meet him there. It became a central place where his devotees could come with a high expectation of having his darshan, and they often succeeded. Previously it was Babaji who was visiting his devotees by going to their places, but henceforth many of them started visiting him. This did not mean that he gave up going to the places he was accustomed to visiting. Even when he began spending the major part of the year at Kainchi, Vrindaban and Allahabad, his roving habit continued. This was necessary, of course, to keep his promise to his devotees, "Yad karane se ham ajate hain." [I come to you when you remember me.]

Once, while taking our morning tea, two cars stopped at the gate. The queen mother of Vizianagram had arrived with her secretary and attendants. She asked whether Babaji was here. When I told her that he wasn't, she broke down crying and exclaimed, "What shall I do now? We have been driving since 2:00 a.m. and have not slept the whole night. Where shall I find him?"

It was difficult to console her. "Mataji, you are tired. Please come rest for a while. Who knows, Babaji may come."

She said she had to return for an appointment with the Finance Minister of India in Delhi at 4:00 p.m. She had come seeking Babaji's advice on some tax problems and estate duties. Finally she agreed to rest and a cot was placed on the verandah for her.

She asked me to narrate some of Babaji's lilas which had occured in the house. The members of her party gathered around and I started talking. After an hour, Babaji suddenly arrived. She fell at Babaji's feet, saying that she had been remembering him all the time so he had come. Babaji took her to his room and told her what to do and say in her upcoming meeting. He explained everything in detail, ending with "Sab thik ho jayega." [All will be well.]

She was entirely a changed person, as if by some magic touch. She was given some milk and fruits. There would be no problem reaching Benares in time for her son to fly her in his plane to the meeting in Delhi.

The persons who had come with Babaji told us of his sudden decision last evening to return to Allahabad. He had arrived in Nainital that morning and the devotees there expected he would stay at least for a couple of days. They were all surprised when he suddenly asked a devotee to drive him to Allahabad, a journey of several hundred miles. He said it was very important to travel all night so he could reach Allahabad, where a devotee in distress was remembering him. When the lady heard that, she said with tears in her eyes, "That is Babaji. He knew how I was feeling and how I was crying for his help."

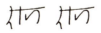

Maharajji and devotees at Kainchi Ashram entrance.

V

KAINCHI

After the Kainchi ashram was built, Babaji began spending the summer months there. In 1964, when some devotees were going there, I was asked to accompany them. I explained that I had to stay back because Babaji might visit at any time. When the devotees got to Kainchi, Baba asked what my reply had been when invited to come to Kainchi. Then Babaji said, "Dada cannot leave his house because of my unscheduled visits. But those who are near to me do not bother about me."

In May 1966, we received a letter from Babaji, who was already in Kainchi, asking us to come as soon as the university closed. Didi and I reached there within a week. This was our first visit. Babaji was waiting for us in his room. While sitting with him, a devotee brought a basket of various kinds of fruits from his garden. Babaji took out some of the fruits and showed me which I might eat and which I should avoid. After I had my tea and prasad, he took me around the ashram.

It took only a few days to get acquainted with the routine going on in the ashram. After getting up early in the morning (we did not know if Baba slept at night or not) and finishing his toilet, Babaji would take a little tea, which was actually more milk than tea. At about eight o'clock he would come out and give darshan, either to groups or to people individually in his small room or visit this and that part of the ashram. After giving darshan and meeting people, Babaji would retire for his bath and food at around eleven o'clock. After finishing a very modest meal, he would be just inside the room, seeing the Mothers or some of the ashramites. But if somebody came with some problem, or was remembering him, he would immediately rush out of the room, in spite of the protests of the Mothers. He would come because the call of the devotees was much more important than his personal comfort or rest. Then at about four o'clock in the afternoon, he would come out again for about four or five hours, until he retired to his room at about eight-thirty or nine in the evening.

When he was visiting Bombay and South India, Baba sent some of the devotees who were accompanying him to an ashram near Bombay to have darshan of the head of that ashram. They returned saying there were fixed hours when darshan was given and they had arrived too soon. Many other visitors waited, but they had left. The same thing was repeated when they visited Bangalore. Babaji sent them to an ashram for darshan, and again they arrived before the fixed hours and left. Baba said to Siddhi Didi, "Look, every sadhu has fixed visiting hours when he gives darshan in his ashram. But you and Dada do not allow me to fix up any time. You always push me out to give darshan to the people at whatever time they arrive." She did not reply.

When we first arrived there was a big tent for a *yagna* that was being celebrated. Many priests were engaged in doing the puja, and the number of visitors was increasing daily. Bhandara was going on—everyone was fed or offered prasad to carry away with them. Everyone was happy, but there were some exceptions.

One day a few political leaders came after visiting some cities in the area. They were welcomed and offered prasad, but their reaction was hostile. Seeing so much *ghee* and other ingredients being used for *havan* and the large number of people being fed *puris*, some of them flared up and said to me, "There is such a food shortage in this country and so many are faced with famine. It is a sacrilege to waste so much food. How this can happen in an ashram is beyond our understanding."

Babaji was not there at the time. Later he asked me about the episode. He said, "These are the persons who have become the guardians of the people. They do not know where the food comes from. They do not take the name of God, offer any puja or perform havans. How will the rains come and produce food? They forget God and think everything depends on them. The whole defect lies there."

One day it was getting to be time for his food, but the devotees kept coming, one after another. Everyone was welcome. The Mothers came to me, "Dada, it is past eleven-thirty. You must take Babaji inside now. It's time for his bath and food." But what could I do? He himself was allowing everyone to come, listening to each with patience and interest. "Dada, it is one o'clock." Siddhi Didi was standing on the other side of the door, beckoning me. I tried to lift Baba up by catching hold of his hand, but he would not budge. He only smiled and looked at me and kept on talking to the people, knowing full well how agitated we were becoming.

After one o'clock, I bolted one side of the door to the room, so that only one door was open. After those who were already in the room left, I bolted the other door. I made him stand up and said, "These people are coming to you after taking their food. They are asking you all the same kinds of questions: about jobs or promotions or transfers, or their children's marriages or examinations, or their husband's drinking and wasting money, or their illnesses—all their worldly and domestic problems!"

I was thinking especially about one old woman who was sitting there and wouldn't move out. She was asking, "Baba, my daughter-in-law has got four daughters, now she must have a son!"

Maharajji replied, "Wherefrom shall I get this son?"

"Baba, your grace, your ashirbad, can get it."

I was very agitated and told him, "Baba, these people are thinking only of their tiny problems without caring at all about you, that you must also need to take a bath and have your food."

He caught hold of my hand, smiled at me, and said, "Dada, you should not be angry. This is the world, this is samsara [illusion]. Nobody comes to me for my own sake; everybody comes for their own problems."

However, here also there were exceptions. The head of the Goraknath sect came to Kainchi one morning. The Goraknaths are a very great sect of sadhus in India and its head was a very powerful and influential man. He came and sat in Babaji's room. Babaji said to me, "Dada, Mahant Digvijaynath is a great saint, touch his feet." I did that. When some other people came, he also told them to touch Mahant Digvijaynath's feet.

The third time Babaji said this, Mahant Digvijaynath stood up and said, "Baba, you who are the saint of saints is sitting before me, and you are making others touch my feet?"

We were sitting with Maharajji near the front of the ashram when a sadhu came walking in the gate. He had a big *jata* and a beard, was wearing *rudhraksha* beads and carrying a trident. As soon as he saw the man, Babaji jumped up and ran toward him. Babaji met the man, spoke to him for a minute or two, and then the man disappeared. He just disappeared! Usha Bahadur cried, "Who was that person?" Maharajji never said a word about it.

One night after the gate was closed and all the guests had retired, I was going around checking that things were all right. I was surprised to see a stranger come walking towards me from the back, the river side of the ashram. He said, "I need a lantern. Can you give me one?"

I said that of course I could and got it for him. Then I asked, "How did you get here this late at night?"

He said, "I was going by truck, but it broke down. Therefore I have come to get a lantern. Don't worry, I shall return the lamp. You can go on with your work."

The next morning Maharajji said to me, "You met *Sombari Maharaj?*" I said no, him I had not met. "The man who took the lantern from you last night, you didn't understand who he was?"

One night, the full moon was just coming up and the whole mountain was illuminated. Maharajji said, "Dada, this is Gargachala." Gargachala means the place where Garga lived. Garga, like Brighu and Vashista, was a very great *rishi*. He used to live and do his *tapasya* on that mountain.

Knowing the rishis are immortal, I asked, "Baba, can we sometimes have a vision of him? Can one see him here?"

He said, "Of course, sometimes he can be seen."

Some time later we were sitting with Babaji in the front room and saw a light on the opposite hill, a great illumination. We were very much excited. Babaji asked, "What are you seeing? What are you seeing?"

We said, "Baba, look! There is so much light!"

"Only light? You cannot hear the bell?" We could not. He said, "Well, well, Garga, you have given them the vision to see, but now you must give them the power to hear." Then he just said, "Jao, jao, jao," and the matter ended there.

When I first went to Kainchi the construction of the main buildings was over, but there were few bathrooms and latrines. For his morning toilet, Babaji used to go into the fields, several furlongs away. Moti Ram and I would accompany him in the jeep. After finishing his toilet, Babaji would sometimes sit by the river; then returning to the road he would sit on the parapet giving darshan.

One day while Baba was sitting on the parapet, Mr. Chavan, the Defense Minister of India, was returning from Ranikhet with a large number of army officials. He was riding by in his car, and when he saw Babaji, he came out and prostrated before him. "Baba, it has been six years since I last had your darshan. This has been a very difficult time for us—there was the trouble with China and then the war with Pakistan."

The army officials, including a general, were gathered around Baba. Babaji said, "India is the land of gods. Nobody can take it by war and conquest. But if politicians give away the land in political games, who can prevent that?" Pointing to the soldiers standing there, he continued, "These are the people who have fought for the country. I went to the war fronts in Kashmir and other places and saw for myself what a fine job they were doing." Prasad was brought from the ashram and then Baba asked them to go.

Although people were getting darshan at all times, the mystery of it remained the same. We realized that getting his darshan depended entirely on him. If he did not want to give it, one would have to be disappointed.

Once we had gone to the train station with Babaji to see him off. The train was late and he sat on the open platform, away from the people. Someone came and told him that a minister of the central government and some members of parliament were here and requested his darshan. Babaji rebuked the messenger, saying they were big "badmash" and he would not meet them. Before the train came, he started walking along the platform, holding my hand. He passed several times in front of the group that had wanted his darshan, but they never saw him.

One day Babaji and I had gone out for a while. When we returned, we saw a number of police constables posted on the ashram premises. The District Magistrate said that Mr. Nanda, the Home Minister, was coming the next morning to meet Babaji. Baba said, "Mr. Nanda can come, but the police must go. This ashram cannot be turned into a prison."

The D.M. said the police could be withdrawn only by government order. Baba asked him to send a telegram to Mr. Nanda telling him not to come to the ashram, but the D.M. said it was not in his power to do that. Babaji had Haridas send the telegram and Mr. Nanda did not come.

A governor of the state tried several times to see Babaji, but did not succeed. He was not coming as a devotee, but in his official position. He ultimately realized why he had missed darshan, and eventually did get to see Babaji.

Another political leader came to Babaji and while he sat there Baba said to me, "Dada, he is such a generous man, such a large-hearted man. I have never come across a person like this! He is almost like a god!" But after the man went away, Babaji said, "He wanted to fool me. I am fooling the whole world, and he came to fool me!"

In 1966 there was an All-India Vice Chancellors Conference in Nainital, to which Vice Chancellors from different universities in India and Nepal had come. Having heard about Maharajji, they all came to the Bhumiadhar temple on Sunday to see him. They sat in Babaji's room and he talked with them. Their whole attention was focused on asking Babaji about the nature of his *sadhana,* who his guru was, what tapasya he had done, and that sort of thing. They were questioning Baba for more than an hour, but he had a nice way of escaping—smiling and replying, but not disclosing anything.

After their darshan, Babaji told me to go and give them prasad. They accosted me and asked what kind of spiritual power or realization Baba had attained. I said I did not know. They would not believe me and insisted I must know these things. But I told them I was not only ignorant, but completely indifferent. They asked why I stayed so close to him. I said, "The reason is this: whenever I am with him, I get so much of peace and joy that I forget everything."

After these gentlemen left, Mr. Mehrotra and Jiban, who had been listening, said, "You have always escaped like an eel from our questions, but today you were well-caught."

I said, "Look here, what great fun it was. These highly educated people heckled Baba for more than an hour, but they could not extract anything. When they asked me what the greatest thing was about Baba, I could not tell them. But to you I can say that he is the greatest bluffer! He has kept everybody in darkness about himself."

Why he did or did not give darshan is difficult to understand. Often he would go out of his way to wait for his devotees. Once he was lying by the roadside in Mussorie in order to give darshan to Mr. K. M. Munshi, the Governor of Uttar Pradesh, who was to pass that way. In 1942 he was sitting on the open platform at the Allahabad train station to give darshan to the retired General McKenna, who was to pass the station in a special army train. In 1971 he was at the Magh Mela ground, waiting for Ram Dass and his party who were visiting that place on their way to Vrindaban in search of Maharajji.

One day he came out of the ashram in Vrindaban and sat on the road, which was full of dust and cow dung. He said this would be a protection from the crowd—no one would sit there for fear of making their clothes dirty. He himself had no such fear. Once he sat on human excreta and soiled his blanket. I had to rush to the ashram to get a blanket and then make him change.

We often felt that he had no consciousness of his body and cared little for its comforts. He would give darshan anytime day or night. Even in the last few years when the stream of visitors increased, with few exceptions he would meet everyone. But some persons did not have darshan no matter how they tried. Several times I asked him to give darshan to some persons who were visiting and he would cut me short, "Dada, you do not understand. They do not come for my darshan, but to test me. They are not interested in me, but in the magic that I am supposed to perform."

The saints choose different ways of doing their work. Babaji chose a life neither of a householder nor of a mendicant. He did not carry any of the outward signs that he was a sadhu or saint—no beads, no long beard, no saffron robes. No one could tell by looking at him that he was a saint. As we learned, even his name seemed to have changed from place to place. The name by which we all knew him was Neem Karoli Baba (that is, the baba from Neem Karoli), but the correct words are Neeb Karori and perhaps give some indication of who that person was. Neeb means foundation and Karori means strong and firm: strong and firm foundation.

When Babaji first came to Nainital, Almora and other hill places, many of the menfolk were meeting him and he visited their houses. There the women, the Mothers, came to know him. But before there were temples and ashrams, there were few places where the women could be with him. He would not take them with him when he roamed about, nor had they the freedom or means to travel to see him. When the ashrams came to be built, these Mas would be coming in the morning and going away in the evening. These ladies were very religious-minded and they found Baba so sympathetic, kind and generous. He made it possible for them to spend so much time with him.

Maharajji was a father to his devotees, a guru of householders. His entire energy seemed to be directed toward our welfare, elevation, and development. He taught ideal social and family life, and showed us that real love and affection, real brotherhood, does not come only from blood relations. There were so many differences among the devotees—caste, language, nationality—usually very

great barriers in India. But here were Kashmiris, Gujaratis, south Indians, north Indians, Westerners—all part of his great family. He broke down the walls and removed the curtains of prejudice. In this family, we could be closer than with our real brothers and sisters.

He would say, "You have great regard and love for the Ganges and all the holy rivers, but you do not live on the bank of the Ganges. You live by a small stream: your house is there, you bathe and wash your clothing there, just as you would in the Ganges. But have this attitude: as the Ganges has come from him, so also has this stream come from him. It is the same water exactly; it is also holy. It will do the same thing."

Maharajji said that the family unit was the most important in society. He encouraged happy family life, love, brotherhood and affection. If each family became disciplined and followed the teachings of the elders and religion, life would be healthy and peaceful. But this could not be controlled and regulated by law.

He said that householders cannot be renunciates. If the householders would leave the home, leave the family and society, the country could not sustain them. The country needed the continuity of creation and work in the world. So he would tell us, "Feed the sadhus, give them money, give them blankets, whatever they need. They do not farm, they do not earn money, you must look after them. It is the householders' responsibility."

There were some politicians who thought that the sadhus were parasites. There were so many *lakhs* of sadhus that had to be supported by society. They seemed to lead a prosperous life, although they did not work and earn. These politicians suggested that the sadhus be drafted to work in hospitals or schools. But Maharajji said, "What do sadhus know of such things? It would be their downfall. The politicians do not know the value of the sadhus and saints. Whatever their faults, they are keeping the lamp lighted, keeping the spirit living. As soon as the sadhus come in contact with money, with property, with business, that is their downfall. And their downfall is the ruination of the entire society."

Prabhudatt Brahmachari, that saint who has his ashrams in Allahabad and in Vrindaban, became rather well-known because he was leading the agitation about cow protection and clashed with the government. Maharajji told him that a sadhu should not become involved in political agitation, "A sadhu's work is *bhajan* and kirtan, puja and prayer. He should not go in for politics."

The great sadhu, Karpatriji, led a religious movement for purification of temples and ashrams and the removal of Muslim mosques that had been constructed over the ruins of Hindu temples. He was also leading an agitation against the new law that permitted untouchables to enter the temples.

One day he came to Maharajji and said, "Such sacrilege is being done! You are a pillar of Hindu society. You must give your support and help us."

Maharajji was furious and told him, "In what way are you a sadhu? You do not go to the temple; you do not do your prayer and puja and bhajan. You are leading this agitation? I have seen some of the temples, there is no one to look after them. I have seen the dogs coming and urinating on the lingams! This is what you want to protect? Those people who want to do puja and prayer, you want to stop them? You do not go, but you want to prevent those who want to go?" Later, when he had calmed down, he added, "This is not the work of a sadhu, this is the work of the politicians. You should keep aloof from it."

A sadhu came to Kainchi one noon, when Maharajji was resting in his room. He wanted Maharajji informed that he had come. The boys who were there said, "We shall ask Dada."

I said, "No, no. If Maharajji is to come out, he will come out on his own. We can go and bring him only at four in the afternoon."

The sadhu said something rather harsh, the boys got furious, and hot words were exchanged. While this was going on, Maharajji came out. Maharajji put a hand on the sadhu, "You have become a sadhu? You failed your school examinations, you stole the ornaments from your family's house, and you ran away. After that you went to Germany and became a very learned person. When you were not able to get suitable employment, you left. That is how you have become a sadhu. I know your father, I know your family. Now you come here quarreling?"

The sadhu was given prasad, but he only wanted to escape. After he had gone, Maharajji said, "Dada, you should rebuke the boys.

They must not quarrel. They should have regard for the clothes that a sadhu wears. They cannot recognize a true sadhu, so it is better for them to show respect."

Many persons have asked me how it was that Babaji frequently said that kamini and kanchan [women and gold] were the deadliest enemies and yet he was in the company of so many women, even in the ashrams and while travelling.

When Babaji travelled to Madras in 1973, he stayed in the Sindhi *dharmashala.* While he was there, Hukemchand was told by one of his friends that a great saint had come. Hukemchand was a lover of saints and so went to the dharmashala. There he found a sadhu sitting on the upper floor giving a discourse, surrounded by many persons. Hukemchand left not very impressed. When his friend asked if he had met the saint, Hukemchand said, "Of course, I saw that sadhu on the upper floor. He was not much to bother about."

The friend said, "No, no. That is not the saint. He is on the ground floor near the staircase."

So Hukemchand returned. There he found a fat old man sitting on a cot, but there was no indication that he was a saint or sadhu. The door to the next room was open and there were ladies talking and attending to him from there. The sight was obnoxious to Hukemchand—that a saint or sadhu was in the company of women and taking their services. He started to leave, but then suddenly turned back and fell at the feet of that person.

Now what charm was applied by Baba so as to convert a more than middle-aged, intelligent and sensible man? Somehow he realized that Babaji could be in the company of any number of women and not be harmed. Hukemchand became a very great devotee.

Babaji was surrounded in Kainchi by so many women. He gave them his ashirbad and let them rub his legs as did any male devotee. But he called all older women "Ma" and all younger ones "Baita" [daughter]. When Radha came with Ram Dass and the other Westerners, Maharajji got down from his cot, bowed to her, touched her feet, and said, "Dada, she is my mother. You also bow at her feet."

Now was it just for show, or was it genuine feeling coming from his heart? When all these persons were sitting around him, Indian and foreigners, men and women, young and old, his sight was not obstructed by the outer vestures of the body or the mind—he saw beyond to the soul.

VI

HANUMAN DARSHAN

Then, of course, there was another type of darshan. One day in the early sixties, Babaji came out of his room and he looked like Hanuman. I had heard from so many devotees that Babaji was an incarnation of Hanuman, but Didi and I still had our doubts. The next day, Maharajji asked Didi to scratch his back. She found his body to be so bulky, so big, that she was actually perspiring while trying to reach her hand across his back.

In 1968, Didi did not go to Kainchi during the summer; she was in Allahabad with her mother, so I came alone. It was the day of the June fifteenth bhandara, the anniversary of the inauguration of the ashram. After taking his food, Maharajji went around the ashram checking on all the activity and visitors. Afterward he went to the riverside and sat on the wall. He talked about an old devotee from Unnao: "He is an old man now, but people say he was the leader of the *dacoits,* taking money from the rich and distributing it to the poor. He defended the helpless although he terrorized stronger people. He used to carry two revolvers, one licensed, the other not. I told him that he should surrender one. He read the *Ramayana* very well. He used to read it for me."

Then I.C. Tewari, an old devotee who has since died, said, "He's the person whom Babaji once asked to read the *Ramayana*. When he asked, 'Baba, wherefrom shall I read?' Baba said, 'Read from the part where I am talking to *Vibishan.*'"

After that we were walking around and Babaji caught hold of my hand. When he did that I would sometimes experience such a heavy pressure that I felt my hand would break. He was leaning so heavily on me, I was afraid that if I fell down, he would also. It was early afternoon and we came before the mandir where many people were sitting. Babaji sat before the Shiva temple, my hand locked in his. He said, "Baitho, baitho." [Sit, sit.] I wanted to extricate myself, but could not.

There were a number of persons whom I knew sitting there—Vrindaban Baba (the old Hariakhan Baba's successor) and many others. Now I was feeling as if I were suffocating, as if my breathing were coming to an end. My hand was so tight in his grip that there was no question of getting free. Then I saw, not Babaji, but a huge monkey sitting there, long golden hair over the whole body, the face black, the tail tucked under the legs. I saw it clearly. I closed my eyes, but still I saw it. After that, I don't know what happened.

At ten o'clock that night, I found myself sitting alone down by the farm. Purnanand, from the tea shop, came and said, "Dada, here you are. We have been searching for you all evening." He took me back to the ashram.

Babaji had not gone inside his room yet; he was sitting on a cot and many devotees were around him. As soon as we came across the bridge and near the temple, somebody said, "Baba, Dada has come." He just said, "*Accha*, thik hai." [Very good.] There was nothing to take notice of, nothing to be excited about. I was feeling very depressed. I didn't want to talk; I just wanted to be alone and go to bed.

The next day Gurudat Sharma and Siddhi Didi and others kept asking me what had happened. They told me that we had been sitting there in front of the Shiva temple, surrounded by many people, when suddenly we were both missing. Then Baba and I were seen walking on the top of the hill. An hour or two later, Baba returned alone. I knew what I had seen—that it was actually Hanuman. It was not a dream, not a mistake. How the time passed, I do not have any recollection.

The next day the normal routine started again. On the third day, I was alone with Babaji in his room. I said, "Now look here, Baba. I am not interested in your miracles. I have had enough. I know you are Baba and that is all I need."

This was the end of a stage in my journey. Now I had come to accept that Babaji was more than a human being—that he was superhuman, a divine incarnation. When I would think about him in this light, new difficulties arose. Being what he is, why did he go out of his way to show us his grace, his compassion, his help and assistance? For me, there was no question of asking him for anything, at least not for myself. I would act as the spokesman on behalf of many of the Mothers, the Westerners, and other persons, but I never asked

anything for myself. Babaji would say, "Dada, what do you want?"
"Nothing."
"Tell me, what do you want?"
"Baba, nothing."
"Tell me, I know what is in your mind."
"So why are you asking me then?"
He said, "Oh, I was just asking."

From the first contact I had with him in 1935, and during the second stage from 1955 when I came to know him, I resisted him. He took so much time, but he never gave up or abandoned me. After having his darshan as Hanuman in 1968, whatever doubts I had cleared away and my whole perspective changed. I was not afraid; I would speak openly and frankly to him. One day Mr. Barman told me, "Dada, you can talk so easily to him, but we are frightened."

I said, "What is there to be frightened of? We make mistakes, we make blunders, but he is so very indulgent, so very forgiving, he doesn't mind our lapses. Doesn't he know what is in my mind, what I am going to do? If it were wrong, or unworthy, he should have checked and prevented it in advance. Is it not so? Therefore, I am not frightened."

From the beginning at Kainchi, Maharajji had the Hanuman temple, a *Lakshmi-Narayana* temple, and a Shiva temple. Much later a *Devi* temple was built. He told me, "Dada, the people in the hills do not accept and worship Hanuman-ji as God. They say he is nothing but 'monkey, monkey.' They are devotees of the goddess, Devi. So long as there is not a Devi temple in the ashram, many will not come. But there is a difficulty in that the people often sacrifice goats in their Devi puja." So he had a Devi temple built there, but it was called Vaishnavi Devi, the devi that does not touch meat or take sacrifice.

The murtis of Hanuman and the other gods and goddesses are considered to be alive. But how do they come to be alive? In Bengal, at *Durga* Puja and *Kali* Puja, murtis are made of clay, straw and bamboo sticks. In my childhood days in the village, I would help in collecting clay and gathering straw for the elders to make the murti. The last stage was painting and dressing. When the murti was to be installed as Devi, the priest came and did the ceremony,

Hanumanji murti, Vrindaban Ashram.

pranpratishta, that is, bringing pran [the life breath]. Until then it is not Devi, just a statue. The puja brings breath, making it alive, and it becomes Devi herself. The mantra has made it living. But the love and devotion of the devotees also make the murti live. Hanumanji and the others would be just statues if they had not been consecrated and made alive by devotion and love.

In Allahabad, near Rambagh Station, there was an old Hanuman temple. Maharajji used to call the Hanuman murti there "Controller General." He often sent people to see it, saying, "Go and meet Controller General." It was a very old temple on a high pedestal with narrow stairs and not much space, so a new temple was proposed. Ojhaji was on the committee, along with Mr. Barghav, and they came to discuss the project with Babaji. They thought there should be a new murti also, but Babaji said, "No, no. No other murti. Take this Hanumanji there."

Mr. Barghav didn't like the idea, so he said, "Maharajji, I cannot decide this myself. I shall put it before the committee."

After some time, Barghav came and said the committee did not approve; the old murti was to be left and a new one installed. Maharajji said, "Thik hai, if Hanumanji wants, he will come there himself." A few days later, the old temple collapsed and, although the murti fell down, it was not harmed. There was then no alternative but to install it in the new temple.

One morning, Maharajji, Mr. Barman and I started to drive to the newly constructed Hanuman temple in Kakriaghat, not far from Kainchi. The river which ran beside the road was in high flood stage and was saffron-colored from all the sand in it. We reached a place where the flood waters had covered the road with sand and our car became stuck.

Babaji said to me, "Chalo, I must urinate." To Barman, Baba said, "Don't worry, someone will come and get us out." After an hour, we returned and found that the car had been removed from the sand by some boys. We started back to Kainchi and came to a depression full of water. Maharajji said, "Take the name of Hanuman. Take the name of Hanuman." We drove safely through the water, but as soon as we made it across a big slab of rock crashed down onto the road behind us. Babaji cried out, "Hanumanji has saved us!"

I happened to glance at Maharajji's hands and noticed that his palms were bright red.[1] Barman also noticed, but I motioned him to keep silent.

Back at the ashram, Vikram Soni had been waiting with a car to take us to an appointment with the Sonis in Bhowali. Seeing him, Babaji began abusing me, saying, "You made us so late. You did not remind me we were to go." While at Soni's bungalow in Bhowali, Maharajji had taken his food and lay on a bed, telling me to sit beside him. Mrs. Soni saw that the soles of his feet were very red. Thinking Babaji was asleep, she asked me to come to the other room to talk about it. As I started to get up, Maharajji shouted, "Where are you going? Stay here!"

Back at Kainchi that evening, the Mothers noticed how red his feet were. When asked, Maharajji said, "I was walking in the sand. That is how they got so red. If you do not believe it, ask Dada."

When they asked me, I said, "Of course it is true. But I was also walking on the sand. Look at my feet, they are not red."

Babaji shouted, "Oh, Dada is in league with you. No one believes me."

In March 1972, two days before the *Holi* celebrations, Babaji told me, "Ask your friend to engage a taxi for us. We start for Amarkantak tomorrow morning at six. The taxi must be suitable for a long journey." My friend returned in the evening saying the taxi had been engaged. Babaji told him the taxi was not a good one, but he argued that it was indeed praiseworthy.

The taxi arrived the next morning. Siddhi Didi, Jivanti, Ganesh and I were ready. While getting into the taxi Babaji said, "It is not the right taxi." The driver and the others argued, "There is nothing wrong with it." We all got in and started.

All through the journey Babaji was saying the taxi would not reach Amarkantak. The ladies were worried. After going for 35 miles, Babaji said we must return. It was a great disappointment and the Mothers began pressing me to ask Baba not to return. But we turned around and started back. Suddenly Babaji asked the driver to turn to the road going left, heading for Chitrakut.

---

[1] The palms of Hanuman's hands and the soles of his feet are bright red.

Babaji was talking to me all the time, the others were silent. It was late in the day. We had about 10 miles more to go to reach Chitrakut. Suddenly a heavily loaded truck collided with the taxi and the engine was smashed. The taxi and truck were locked with each other. A large number of people gathered around and started wondering about our miraculous escape. The taxi driver was fighting with the truck driver for the loss of his taxi, although it was actually the fault of the taxi driver. The truck driver said, "You are fighting for your money, which comes and goes, but think of how your life has been saved. There must be some divine being sitting in your car."

We were not thinking of our own escape. There had been a big jerk, but no physical injury to any of us. When all the quarrels and arguments started outside, Babaji suddenly said, with some excitement in his voice, "How Hanuman has saved you all! He has saved your lives, but He has also spared me from a great punishment. How could I have faced Ma, Maushi Ma and Kamala if I had returned alone? The Mothers would have asked me, 'Baba! Where have you left our sons and daughters?' Kamala would have said, 'Baba, what have you done to me?'" It was a very memorable thing to see him so stirred and talking of Hanuman's grace.

The taxi was tied to the back of a truck and we reached Chitrakut, staying in Shiva's temple with Ram Roshan Baba. The ladies began preparing food and arranging beds. The river was in front of the temple. Babaji and I sat out on the ghat. It was a full moon night and everything was bathed in moonlight. Peace and serenity reigned everywhere. Babaji said, "Dada, you are liking this place. This is a sacred place. You can breathe the air and feel how everything is sanctified here." It was our fifth visit here, but it somehow felt different.

The next morning was Holi. Many sadhus gathered around Babaji and Ram Roshan Baba. Babaji asked me to get *jaleebis* and sweets, but Ram Roshan took the money from me and said he would get them. The Mothers told me to ask Babaji to take us to Hanumandhara. I said, "He makes his own decisions and I never interfere." But we did go to Hanumandhara.

It was a long journey, with dust, thorns and pebbles. Babaji was in a dandi and I was walking beside him. The ladies and Ganesh, with the food basket, were coming behind. We reached the foot of the hill, which began a very stiff climb up narrow, high steps. As we climbed, Babaji was talking and talking. All my attention had to be there and not for my own safety. Suddenly the dandiwallahs stopped, shivering and perspiring. They all gazed at their passenger. "Who is he? The dandi has become so very heavy!" As they started climbing again, the burden became light. In everyone's hearing, Babaji said, "Dada, Hanumanji came here and pacified himself after burning Lanka." Then bringing his mouth closer to my ear, he said in a whisper, "Hanuman to hamesha santa rahe." [Hanumanji was always at peace.]

What a jewel he had cast! It was the key not only to Hanuman, but also to himself. All the shouting and joking were like the waves on the surface of the ocean. But in the depths of that ocean all was calm, all tranquil, all peaceful. He was living in that peace and serenity all the time.

We reached the foot of the Hanuman murti, carved out of the hill with a stream flowing at his feet. Babaji was moving around, showing me the place and talking. Suddenly he asked, as if waking me up, "Dada, are you liking it, are you enjoying it? The Mothers are badmash. They wanted us to go to Amarkantak. How could I go when Hanumanji has called me here?"

March 1972 was to be the last time Babaji physically stayed in Allahabad, although we did not know it. As usual, there was much activity, many people coming and going every day. One evening he said, "Dada, there will be *Sundarakand* tomorrow afternoon. Ask Ma and Maushi Ma and Kamala to finish with feeding everyone so that by two o'clock there can be the Sundarakand."

Rajuda, Mukund and other persons were there and they said, "Dada, don't worry, we shall arrange it."

I answered, "What is there to worry about? Hanumanji himself will be there, he will arrange everything."

Later that evening my nephew Vibouti returned from his evening walk with a picture that a restaurant keeper in the Civil Lines area had given him. It was a calendar with a picture of Hanumanji on it. I took it and automatically removed the calendar part from it. While I was doing so, Maharajji said, "Dada, what is that? Bring it to me." He looked at it and said, "Hanumanji has got lost; I also have

Maharajii and Dada with calendar picture of Hanuman on shelf.

got lost. Put it up in the hall for the Sundarakand tomorrow." But twice or thrice he asked to see it again before it was put up. He said that after the Sundarakand it was to be framed and kept in the room.

While we were talking I asked him, "Baba, shall we invite this person, shall we invite that person?"

He shouted at me, "Is it your daughter's marriage that you are going to give invitations? Whoever is to come will come. You are not to invite anybody." But after the storm, the soft showers came and he said gently, "Dada, you don't understand? There will be so many persons that there will be no space in the hall."

The next day all the devotees who were there were fed. Mukund was in charge of playing the harmonium and leading the kirtan. He was expert and efficient in that. Everyone was sitting and waiting for Babaji to come and they wanted me to go and bring him. The *tucket* was empty, waiting for Hanumanji to come and take his seat. I went to his room to bring him. Now when Babaji had first come to Allahabad from Vrindaban in November or December, he was wearing a black blanket. As was her habit, Maushi Ma had a new blanket for him to wear, which she brought to his room. He said, "Maushi Ma, this is a very good blanket. Keep it for a while, I shall wear it afterwards."

They argued back and forth, but Maushi Ma was adamant. "You will not wear it, you will give it to somebody. I shall make you wear it."

So finally he allowed the blanket to be put on and kept it for a few minutes. Then he said, "Maushi Ma, is it all right now? Now give it to Siddhi, I shall wear it afterwards."

Maushi Ma was not fully satisfied, but had to accept it. So I had told Siddhi Didi that when Baba was to go for the Sunderakand, the old black blanket should not be worn. She should put Maushi Ma's chocolate-colored blanket on him. Siddhi said, "You say it as if it is so very easy, but we can't do it. He will push us away and not take it."

When I came to his room, he was sitting on the cot, others were standing around. He said, "Chalo!" and caught hold of my hand. But I stopped and said, "Baba, change this blanket."

"Nahin [No], it is very good!"

"Of course the blanket is very good."

"Then why?"

"Baba, we are going for an auspicious occasion, for a very sacred ceremony, and the black is not considered to be auspicious."

He shouted, "These wretched women! They would not allow me to change it. Maushi Ma has given me a good blanket, I have kept it for today!"

I wish there had been a movie camera to record that entrance. We went into the hall, I was holding that monkey, he was looking this side, looking that side. We two came so slowly, with measured steps. He sat there, everyone was so thrilled, Hanumanji had come.

When the Sundarakand was perhaps halfway through, he got up, saying "Chalo!" It was very disturbing for the singers, but he went out to the feeding area and a cot was placed there for him. He said to me, "You are a fool. You have got those refreshments to give to the people, now the Sundarakand will be over and they will go. When will you give them tea or serve the sweets? Have tea prepared and call them out a few at a time." So he sat on that cot and four or five persons would be called out to take refreshments.

When the Sundarakand was over, the picture of Hanumanji was framed and placed in the hall. He said, "It should not be removed from here." It is there still.

After my experience in Kainchi, when I came to realize that Babaji was himself the incarnation of Hanuman, I became much interested in the life and work of Hanuman. Of course, I had been hearing the *Hanuman Chaleesa,* which the devotees would sing before Baba and at his temples and ashrams. But before that experience, I could not believe that a human being could have the supreme energy, the supreme devotion, the sense of self-sacrifice and self-effacement to be the perfect servant of his lord and preceptor. Ultimately, I found that whatever I came to know about Hanuman was not by reading the Hanuman Chaleesa or the *Ramayana,* but by living in the company of Hanuman himself and his devotees.

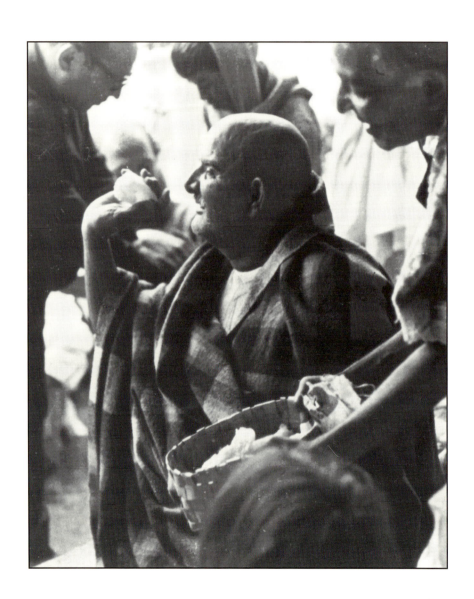

VII

"WHOEVER COMES IS YOUR GUEST"

Maharajji took special care to see that whoever came to Kainchi was given prasad. When I first reached Kainchi, Babaji said, "Dada, whoever comes here is your guest. They come to see Hanumanji with their love and respect and you have got to welcome them. You must receive them properly and serve prasad to all."

Aside from the day-to-day visitors, there would be many who would stay at the ashram for longer periods of time. They were always provided for fully. Babaji would see that no one felt neglected or unattended. He made certain that children and many older devotees were provided with cow's milk. Beds had to be soft and pillows provided. Drinking water was kept in the rooms and flashlights were given to those who had none. The idea was to give the people staying in the ashram all the comforts they were accustomed to getting at home. It reminded me of the *Ramayana*, where so many monkeys came before Ram and he made each one feel that he loved him most.

The food for the ashramites was prepared in a separate kitchen by cooks employed for this purpose and was served by the devotees visiting the ashram. Babaji kept close watch on everyone and everything, down to the tiniest detail. He would visit the kitchens to keep people alert. Early in the morning, as soon as the prasad—puris and vegetables or *halva*—was prepared, he would examine it carefully to see if the right ingredients had been used, if the potatoes were well-cooked, and if the puris were well-fried. He would say that it was of utmost importance to maintain the purity and sanctity of the prasad. On many occasions he blurted out that he had formerly been a "halwai" [confectioner] and he knew how things were to be prepared.

Prasad for the daily visitors was prepared in the kitchen on the back side of the ashram. From there, the puris and vegetables would be brought to the prasad room in the front of the temple and the packets

would be prepared and distributed. At five o'clock when the gates of the ashram were closed, the prasad, the buckets and utensils would be removed back to the kitchen and the room would be cleaned. The first year I was at Kainchi I helped in the preparation—packing the prasad and distributing it. The next year, Maharajji rebuked me, "Are you going to spend all your time doing those things? This can be easily done by others. You should be supervising."

At Kainchi, huge quantities of food were served every day as prasad, in sufficient amounts as to constitute a full meal for the majority of people. Especially in the countryside, hunger is the bane of a large portion of the population. Maharajji would remove the hunger of as many as would come to him. Often he said, "Food is God. Feeding the hungry is actually worship." People were well-acquainted with his statements: "God comes before the hungry as food," and "First bhojan [food] and then bhajan [prayer]."

Sometimes the amount of food prepared seemed to be more than could be distributed, but Babaji always knew how many persons would be visiting and how much prasad was to be served. He would tell me, "Dada, prasad can never be in excess or surplus. It all depends on how you distribute it. There should be no waste or misuse."

People give their money and provisions to Hanumanji. The day they are wasted, they will not give to Hanumanji anymore. This must not be forgotten."

The bhandara would continue openly until five o'clock. Babaji used to make his rounds of the ashram after the gates closed. One day we came to the prasad room and found there was a full basket of puris and two buckets of potatoes that had remained undistributed. The puris could be taken by the ashramites at night, but the potatoes would surely be wasted. The prasad had been distributed by some elderly people. I said, "Couldn't they see by three or four o'clock that they needed to increase the amount of prasad that was distributed?"

Baba looked at me, smiled and said, "Dada, you do not know how very painful it must be to give. They would rather waste and throw away than give to others."

One summer a rich businessman was living in the ashram with his wife and two teenaged children for a month. Seeing how the feeding was done every day, he expressed his interest in feeding sweets to the people visiting the ashram and sought Babaji's permission to do so. He said he would get the required ingredients from the market and the sweets would be prepared in the ashram kitchen. Babaji gave his consent, but he advised me not to get involved.

The *laddus* were prepared and brought before Hanumanji's temple in the morning, but the method of distribution was far from satisfactory. Children were put to various kinds of tests before they were given the sweets. Some were sent to pluck leaves from the forest for serving them. Many children were sent away without any because they were suspected of coming for second or third helpings, no matter how they denied it.

When the day ended and the gates were closed, more than half of the sweets remained undistributed. I told Babaji it was a disgrace for the ashram and he should not have encouraged the project. First he said, "How can I force people to give these things away if they do not want to do so?" I told him that it was entirely against the tradition of the ashram that people should go away without getting prasad. Then he said, "I just wanted to show that it is not easy to do bhandara in the name of Hanumanji. If you give only to the people of your choice, then the food will remain and go to waste. If you

have offered your food to Hanumanji, it no longer belongs to you. Hanumanji himself sees that people get their prasad."

He said to make more sweets in the ashram and do another bhandara, preparing a much larger quantity and distributing to everyone in the real tradition of the ashram. Two days later the laddus were prepared, about fifteen mounds in quantity. Since only the regular visitors would be getting the prasad, some felt part of the sweets would surely remain undistributed. But Babaji's ways of getting things done were unpredictable.

When the sweets were being distributed, some old people and the children started eating them right there. Babaji came several times during the distribution. He said that anyone who wanted to eat the laddus here should be given as many helpings as they could eat. "It is Hanumanji's bhandara. You need not be worried about anybody not receiving prasad."

One old woman began crying, "No one has ever fed me like this before."

By one o'clock the whole supply was exhausted and Babaji went around the ashram shouting, "Dada has distributed the entire prasad!"

Now here was a lesson. If you think that you or I have something, we cannot give. You must think of it as Hanumanji's—that only he can give. You are only the ladle, the leaf on which it is being given.

Those who lived with him in the ashrams saw for themselves how Babaji used to emphasize giving food to the people and being alert about it. He had his way of pulling up people in case of any lapses. Often he did not tell the person concerned directly about it, but would accuse or rebuke someone else in order to teach others. Dada would be very handy in these cases. When someone was putting more food in the packets than could be consumed, Baba would say, "Dada will squander away everything. He doesn't use his brain, but goes on giving away. There is so much wastage of Hanumanji's prasad." After seeing dissatisfaction on the faces of people taking the prasad, Baba would say, "Dada is becoming excessively greedy. He gives so little prasad."

Once in Allahabad, Ma and Maushi Ma were complaining to Babaji that they never had time to sit with him because they were always so busy in the kitchen, cooking the food and feeding the people. Babaji said, "Ma, I am with you in the house all the time. You are not away from me. The work that you are doing—cooking with your own hands and feeding the people—that is the highest sadhana for the householder. You mustn't think you are missing anything."

In Allahabad we usually got jaleebis in the morning to give out. Maharajji would be sitting and waiting, "Jaleebis have not yet come?" They would arrive in a bucket and he would distribute them

by handfuls. The problem was that he would be thrusting his hand into the bucket and taking out the sweets to distribute. There had to be water and a towel nearby to wash his hand, otherwise the syrup would be everywhere and Didi would be shrieking.

In Kainchi, jaleebis came from Bhowali every day in the summer. When I distributed, I would go from this side to that side with the bucket. If I did not, they would all be distributed in the front portion of the ashram and the workers in back would not get any. One day someone came and asked, "Where is Dada?"

Babaji said, "Go in back and find the man whom the dogs are following; he is your Dada."

It was said that Purnanand's father, who lived across the road, would watch to see who was coming with what kind of food. When there was something he liked, he would come. One day Babaji said, "Dada gives prasad looking at the faces of the people and gives to his favorites. But I do not do that. I give to everyone."

I said, "You also give to your friends."

"Who?"

"To Purnanand's father. You give him so much of jaleebis."

"Oh, Dada, he is an old man. How long is he going to live? Therefore, I give him so much."

Mangoes were a favorite delicacy of most of the people in Kainchi, but the poorer people could not afford to buy them. Inder and Jiban would send mangoes and we would distribute them. Later there was a serious failure of the mango crop and they became hard to get. In 1972 and 1973, Babaji was giving up so many things: "This I do not eat, that I do not eat . . ." He not only stopped eating sweets, but also many fruits and other delicacies.

In 1973, Inder and his wife came and they had managed to get twenty or thirty choice mangoes. They said, "Dada, take them to Baba."

I said, "Baba will not eat them." But they insisted that I take the mangoes to him. Baba was in his room at nine at night taking a little porridge when I brought the mangoes.

"What do you have, Dada?"

"Mangoes."

"Dada, I do not eat mangoes anymore."

"Then don't eat them."

"Dada, formerly I used to eat two hundred mangoes! I would go to the garden and the gardeners would feed me. I would eat two hundred mangoes."

"What are you saying? You cannot eat two mangoes and you say you used to eat two hundred?"

"If you do not believe me, what can I do?"

Baba liked a sweet called sandesh and said it was good for coughs. Since it was hard to obtain, Didi had the sweetmeat seller prepare one kilo of sandesh to give as prasad. She brought it when she returned from her college at five o'clock. As soon as she arrived, Baba came out of his room. "Kamala, what have you brought? What have you brought?"

She told him, "Sandesh," and showed it to him. He took it and ate one piece after another until not a single bite was left.

In 1971, when so many Westerners came to Allahabad, they took their meals at our house. Every day Maharajji would ask me what food I was going to prepare for them. There had to be ample food for all. When one of the Westerners would protest, "No more sweets," Maharajji would say, "Feed them! Feed them! If they fall ill, call the doctor."

There were many occasions when we saw how very painful it was for Baba when someone had to go hungry.

There was a servant named Khemua in the ashram who used to clean the utensils, sweep and dust the rooms and carry logs and wood. He had a very peculiar way of dressing—in pajama pants, a shirt, and a policeman's cap. He was somewhat unusual and the servants in the ashram would tease him. Sometimes he would shout and retaliate if provoked, but he was a harmless sort of fellow.

He was not interested in his clothes or the food or money that was given to him and wore the same tattered clothes until I gave him some new ones. He became very attached to me and would stop and salute when he saw me. Babaji would say, "Dada goes on lighting a cigarette for himself, puts one in Khemua's mouth and both go on smoking."

Once Khemua quarrelled with the servants in the kitchen and Babaji said, "Khemua, you go away from here. Get out!"

Khemua replied, "I will not go."

"You must get out!"

"When Hanumanji's work is finished, then I shall get out."

Babaji said, "What can I do? He will not go."

Later Khemua was transferred from kitchen work to the ashram farm to look after the cattle. Khemua was not allowed to enter the ashram premises. He would come to the ashram at night and wait outside the gate. It was the duty of the kitchen servants to bring him his food there.

One night there were many people going here and there, the kirtan party was singing, many things were going on. Usually when Babaji came to his room after giving evening darshan, he would take a little food. That night he didn't take any. Some time after one o'clock I was in my bed and the chaukidar came and said, "Dada, Maharajji is calling you."

I went to his room and Siddhi Didi said, "Dada, he has not eaten anything. He is just sitting there like that." Babaji sat with tears flowing from his eyes.

"Dada, Khemua has not taken his food today."

"Hah, Baba, how did that happen?"

"He was waiting at the gate for a long time, but nobody served his food. The servants must have forgotten. He waited and waited, then he went away."

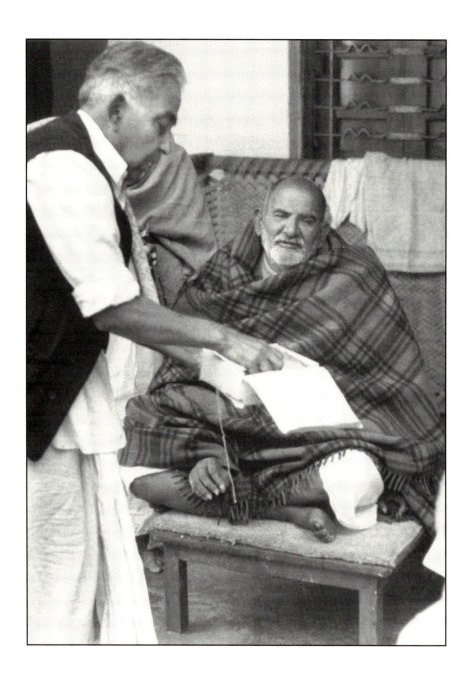

I said, "Then, Baba, shall we go and take his food to the farm?"
"No, no, we cannot do that. He will not eat this late at night."

The next morning when I came into Baba's room, the Mothers had assembled to do their morning puja and *arti* to Maharajji. This used to be their most enjoyable time, worshipping him and relishing his jokes and sallies. But that day it was different. Everyone was standing quietly and shedding tears. Babaji was talking about how very painful it was to keep people starving. What kind of *dharma* was it when people failed to attend to those who depended on them?

There is a small roadside temple of Hanumanji down below Bhowali in Bhumiadhar. The area is mostly inhabited by very poor people belonging to the lower class of untouchables. They did not have any regular source of income, and being illiterate they could not get any desirable employment. The educated and upper classes would not fraternize with them. Only the missionaries visited them sometimes and handed out doles.

Babaji knew their condition very well. Maybe it was to help these people that Babaji built the temple in that location. When he visited the area, the people would always get fed. The educated and upper-class devotees who came to Babaji saw for themselves the pitiable condition of these people and this also resulted in some help for them. Babaji's presence in the temple was a source of hope and expectation for them. Here was someone who loved them and would always be ready to give them help. To him they were not untouchables, and many would surround him when he was there.

One morning Babaji left Kainchi and went to Bhumiadhar. Within a short time many visitors gathered. Since it was a Sunday, many visitors from Nainital, Ranikhet and other places, who had gone to Kainchi to see Maharajji, now came to Bhumiadhar. They were all sitting around him, even occupying part of the road. Some Mothers had brought food cooked for him. He was asked to eat, but he did not agree.

While Maharajji was talking, a shilpakar [a type of untouchable who did menial work] came carrying a glass in his hand and stood on the road. The man's clothes were very dirty and the glass and piece of cloth covering it were no better. Babaji beckoned to him and took the glass from his hand when it was offered. Babaji exclaimed, "Dada, this is amrit. You take it."

I had not attained to that height as to feel very enthusiastic about drinking from that dirty glass offered by that dirty man. I did not feel it was nectar. However, taking the glass, I was going to drink it. Babaji snatched the glass away from my hand, saying, "Dada, I must drink some first." He took a few sips and then offered it to me.

I drank the milk, boiled with such care, as indicated by the thick layer of cream on it. Everyone was amazed and sat silently watching. The caste barrier was broken. Baba could do it, but I could not have done it by myself. Did Babaji drink it to teach something to the people looking disparagingly at this man, who had offered the milk with such love and devotion? Was it to resolve the conflict in my mind which was not unknown to him? It was a token of that unbounded grace which flowed so spontaneously.

It was also in Bhumiadhar one early morning that some visitors came. There were five in the party—a young man and his wife and three small children. I brought them prasad and they were just leaving when Babaji came out of his room. Seeing Babaji, the wife immediately began to narrate her tale of woe. They belonged to the lower class and her husband had little regular income, most of which he used for drink. For the last three days the children had not eaten and she didn't remember the last time she had seen a whole meal. There was nothing in the house that she could sell or pawn to purchase food for her hungry children. Failing at every door, she had come to him.

While the woman was telling her story, Babaji was visibly moved. He told me to bring more prasad. Not satisfied, he asked me to bring a basket filled with puris. Then he asked me to give them some wheat flour, packed in my bedsheet. But how were they going to cook, as they had no utensils in their house? He said to give them some utensils, a lota, pans, etc. They tied up their things and were ready to go. Suddenly, "Dada, give them some money. Do you have some more? Give them twenty rupees more. They are very poor and helpless. They do not live here. When she saw her children were starving without any help, she came here."

It was a memorable sight. So easily is the calm surface of the deep lake agitated when a small piece of stone is thrown in it.

VIII

"IF YOU DO NOT MAKE IT EMPTY . . ."

Babaji had built the ashrams at Kainchi and Vrindaban, but they were not run as ashrams in the strict sense of the term. A visitor unacquainted with his name would take it to be a big household rather than an ashram. Except for a few sadhus who might be staying for a short while, it was the life of the householder that was lived at the ashram. No one was a permanent resident; all were visitors. They came to the ashram for a break from the worries and burdens which go with the life of the average householder.

The life in the ashrams all centered around Maharajji. People came and tried to spend as much time with him as possible. There were certain hours when everyone was sure to see him. Everyone looked to him as the head of the household: it was his responsibility to provide everything for everyone. He took upon himself all their burdens so they could enjoy the happiness of being near him. Many performed various kinds of service out of sheer joy and not from any compulsion.

Sometimes Babaji would say that people living in other ashrams did all kinds of work, even ladies from rich families. But in Kainchi or Vrindaban the work was done by servants. He asked me, "Dada, why do people not work here as in other ashrams?"

I said, "Baba, in those places people go for the purpose of serving, but here people come to the nana's [maternal grandfather's] house for enjoyment."

He said, "Who is the nana here?"

"You are, of course. All fun and no work."

He laughed and repeated, "I am the nana, I am." And he laughed about it all that day.

In Baba's ashrams the storerooms would be full of all the essential things. What was needed, where it was to come from, how the payments were to be made—that was all his responsibility. How he did this was a great mystery. Huge amounts of provisions would be used every day but he would always know the exact inventory, although no records were maintained.

The provisions for the kitchen were purchased on credit from shops at Haldwani and other places. Haridas used to be in charge of ordering supplies and making payments. One day Babaji reminded Haridas that a payment had not been made to a shopkeeper in Haldwani for a long time and shouldn't be delayed any longer. Haridas was certain the shopkeeper was owed 11,000 rupees. Babaji said the amount was less. The next morning Haridas was given the 11,000 rupees and when he left Babaji told me he would only have to pay 7,000 rupees, which was in fact what happened.

Some of the visitors who came to Kainchi wondered where Babaji got his money. They saw bhandara going on all the time and money being spent lavishly. One day, a certain person asked to meet me alone. He had seen me distributing prasad and being close with Babaji and wanted to know where the money came from. He wanted me to testify that Babaji was creating money. Such cases were not rare. They made us realize that all kinds of people came to Babaji with different aims and motives. In this way we could understand when he said, "So many come not for meeting me, but to test me."

Money came from many quarters, but Baba was very selective. He would often say that money came to Hanumanji—it belonged to him. If you used it properly and avoided all misuse and wastage, there would always be enough. We would see him accept money from a devotee who loved to give with no other motive. If there were strings attached, he would reject it outright.

Back in 1966 there was a small wooden bridge over the river in Kainchi, not the big bridge that is there now. He would sometimes go and sit there in the afternoon and take his food. A few days before the June fifteenth bhandara he was sitting there when a devotee from Bareilly came in a truck. He had brought some supplies for the bhandara—a basket of clay cups and two or three packets of leaf plates. He came and sat before Baba and said to me, "Dada, tell me what else is needed?"

"Nothing."

He went on pestering me, "What else? What else?"

Then I said, "All right, if you want to send something, then send another two baskets of those clay cups." Those cups are not easily available in the hills.

Maharajji cried, "What? What are you going to do with them? You have got so many. You are very greedy. Whenever somebody offers you something, you jump for it." I kept quiet.

When the man had taken prasad and was about to leave, he took a hundred rupee note and put it before Babaji. "What is this?"

He said, "Babaji, it is for the bhandara." Babaji took the note, tore it into pieces and threw it into the river. The man gasped, but had no words to say. He went away very sad and disappointed.

Babaji said to me, "You didn't understand? You should never accept money or eat the food offered by a miser. You can never digest that! That man has so much money, but he never gives anything in charity or feeds anybody. I know him well."

One day Baba was giving darshan to some high dignitaries and big businessmen. There was lots of talk about what Nixon was doing, the Indian prime minister, and about the stock market. While discussing the price of gold, Babaji said the price would start falling because Russia would stop purchasing gold on the international market.

A month or so later, an impressive, middle-aged man in a silk kurta [Indian shirt] and white jacket was sitting with some people in Babaji's room. He had been given prasad but was still sitting, and it seemed to me that he was waiting for an opportunity to talk to Babaji alone. When the others had left, he took out a large amount of currency notes and put them on Babaji's tucket.

"What is this?"

"This is for you to use for your bhandara. You have saved me from such a big loss. I am a bullion merchant. I was purchasing gold when the prices were rising. I was actually taking out a loan from the bank to purchase more, but I was here when you said that the price would fall. I sold some of my stock and made a large gain."

Maharajji said, "Accha? Accha?" as if he did not know anything of such matters. Then, "Dada, do you need money?"

"No, Baba."

"I do not need money; Dada does not need money. What shall we do with the money?"

The man said, "Baba, please take it."

But Babaji would not do so. After the man went away he said, "Dada, you must be regretting the loss of so much money." I said this was so. "Dada, what can you take from human beings? What have they got to give you? It is God who gives. God has everything. You did not understand why he was giving the money. That was not an offering to me, but my purchase price. If I had accepted it, then he would have come every time he was making a big deal to get tips from me. He would have thought that he had a claim on me."

But there were many devotees whose offerings Babaji would accept easily, saying they were offerings to Hanumanji for his bhandara. Some would be asked to give money or provisions for the ashram. Many devotees felt that all was given by him and they were only passing back again what was already his.

One day while Babaji was sitting on the porch surrounded by people, a car stopped at the ashram gate. Babaji told me to open the door to his room as this visitor would want to talk to him alone. While going to the room with Babaji, I said that he looked like a pickpocket. Babaji laughed and said, "No, no, Dada. He is going to give you money for your bhandara. He is a great devotee of Hanumanji and often sends money for prasad."

On so many occasions we saw him take money from some and refuse it from others. It was obviously not the money, but the person giving it and what he had in mind. Sometimes other issues complicated the matter. This was the case with money offered by the Western devotees.

Harinam Das was one of the Western devotees in Kainchi in the summer of 1971. He wanted to offer some money to Babaji as a token of his love for him. He proposed writing a cheque in my name, knowing the money would reach Babaji. I had to decline, saying that I could not accept it without Babaji's approval. When we talked to Babaji about it, he said I had done the right thing—money should not be taken from the Westerners.

Harinam Das left the room very upset. Babaji said to me, "Dada, it is not proper to take money from them. They have come from long distances and have spent so much money getting here, they must be discouraged from giving money to me. They are not like you; they offer their money out of a pure heart. But once we start taking it, many persons will ask them for money, which will bring a bad name on this ashram."

The matter did not end there. Harinam Das asked Babaji several times over the summer about the money. Finally Babaji gave his consent and Harinam wrote a cheque for $2,200 in my name. When it was credited I was to send the amount to the ashram. On reaching Allahabad I did as I had been advised and was told by the bank it would take three months to clear the cheque and receive the money.

Four days after that I had a long letter from Babaji telling me that he had thought the matter over and decided the money should be returned. Although I knew full well that I did not have that amount in my account, I sent the cheque as ordered by Babaji.

When I was back in Kainchi in September, Harinam Das came and put my cheque before Babaji, asking him to take it back. To his great disappointment, Babaji did not agree. In Allahabad, I learned that only two days before Harinam had cashed my cheque, his original cheque had been credited to my account—months before it should have been!

Harinam was unhappy about the whole situation, as Babaji well knew. When he was leaving for America, Harinam left the money with Anjani, hoping that some day Babaji might be gracious enough to accept it. When Anjani brought the money to Kainchi, Baba told me that the money should be put in Hanumanji's donation box in the temple. It should be at night when no one would see it being done. He said, "When Anjani puts the money in the box, push it in with a stick. Otherwise the priest has a way of taking it out." So after everyone had gone to their rooms, we went to the temple, went behind the curtain and stuffed the money in the box. It was great fun!

Many of his devotees who brought food, fruits, blankets or clothes wanted Babaji not only to accept the gifts, but also to use them himself. This seldom happened. His wants were few and as soon as these articles came, he usually gave them away.

One exception was when Krishna Das's mother, Sylvia, came from America and brought a very nice pullover for Babaji. He was so delighted, asking where it was made, saying the wool was so very soft, and all those things. "Imagine, she was coming from such a long distance, but she has brought something. Look at the people who are here with me, they would never think of getting anything for me." It was seldom possible to make him take anything, even food, but when this lady brought this pullover, Maharajji not only accepted it, he also showed it to all and wore it.

On the other hand, there was a high Indian official who used to come with his wife to see Baba. Once his wife said to me, "Dada, I want to knit a pullover for Baba. Shall I do it?"

"That is your choice," I told her.

"No, no," she said, "Will he wear it?"

"Of course I don't know if he will wear it."

"No, you have got to make him wear it."

When she insisted that I could make him wear it, I said no one could make him do anything. But she decided to take the risk and make the pullover. When she brought it to Baba he said, "Dada, it is good. Keep it and I shall wear it later."

She said, "No Baba, you wear it now."

But he would not, nor did he ever. He gave it away. He knew the terms and conditions attached to it and what had gone into the making of it.

His clothes were very simple, usually a dhoti and a blanket or white sheet. So also his bed and few other things were the simplest. He was quite at home in the houses of his poorest devotees and relished the modest food offered to him. Living with him one felt that even food was not necessary and he could easily manage with nothing.

After Maharajji would take his daily bath in Allahabad, we would give him a new dhoti to wear. Siddhi Didi said, "There is no need for a new dhoti every day. The same dhoti can be washed and given to him to wear again." But I wanted to do it and Baba seemed to like it.

One day before leaving with some of the devotees he said, "I must change my dhoti." Even though he had changed in the morning, I gave him a new one. When they returned a week later, Babaji was a sight! He had no blanket, no undershirt, only the dhoti, which was wrinkled and covered with dust and cow dung.

I said to those persons, "You wretched people! You are so keen and particular about your own clothes and washing every day, but look at this fellow. What is he wearing?"

They protested, "What could we do? We asked him many times to take a bath and change his dhoti, but he would not do it. He said, 'I shall keep this. I shall not change.'" He had been wearing it for one whole week, sitting anywhere and everywhere, visiting the Jagganath temple, Dakshineshwar and Benares. But no bath, nothing of the sort. That dhoti afterwards was kept by us.

Seeing Baba spending so much money and surrounded by so many things, some people thought he was attached to them. Not only householders made this error, but sometimes sadhus also.

Once in the month of October, when Kainchi was already cold, Babaji was sitting in front of a charcoal stove when a sadhu came and began shouting at him, "So it has come to this. You have accumulated so much wealth that you have forgotten all your sadhana and live like a prisoner. Don't you remember that attachment is the deadliest poison for a sadhu? This was not expected of you." Baba persuaded him to sit and take some prasad. He then asked the sadhu to give him some money. The sadhu said he had none, but Babaji kept pressuring him and reluctantly he took out a few hidden rupee notes.

Babaji kept coaxing him to give more. Babaji went on counting and fondling those notes while looking directly at the sadhu, talking to him. As if by accident, the notes fell on the burning charcoal. Seeing his money burning up, the sadhu jumped up and began abusing Babaji in the strongest terms, "You are swelling with money and therefore you do not attach any value to these notes. You do not know how very precious they are to me. It has taken a long time to accumulate that amount and I have been holding it for my needs."

Babaji kept quiet and reached for some tongs. He began to stoke the fire and started pulling new notes out of the fire and counting them.

Seeing what was happening, the sadhu became quiet. When Babaji offered him the notes back, he became very repentent and apologetic. Babaji said, "You have been saying that sadhus must

not have attachment. How then did that come to you? You were so attached to these few pieces of paper, taking them to be so very precious in the journey of your life. That is not the nonattachment you were preaching." The sadhu sat silent a long time, took his prasad, and left.

In Kainchi and Vrindaban and also in Allahabad, Maharajji would have me distributing money, "Give him so much, give her so much." The money would be in the pocket of my black vest. When that money was gone, I would go and take more from Didi's box. Sometimes Maharajji would give me some, "Here, take this money, you will spend it." From the very beginning there was no question of whether I was spending my money or the money that came from his hand.

One day the money in my pocket was gone and I was going for more. Jiban Baba was waiting outside the room and, knowing where I was going, he gave me a bunch of notes. He had done this on a number of occasions. When I returned to the room Baba said to me, "Dada, if you do not make it empty, how are you going to fill it up again?"

Maharajji would give all kinds of things as prasad, including blankets. Once a sadhu came who was going to Badrinath and he was to be given a blanket. The blankets in the storeroom were all gone. Baba said, "Dada, what will you do now?"

"Oh, I will give him a blanket." I went to my room and took a blanket from there.

Maharajji said, "That blanket is not yours! That is Kamala's blanket."

I said, "What of that? She will not mind."

"Accha? She will not mind? You are giving her blanket?" Later Babaji said, "Dada, a devotee from Barielly has just sent you a big bundle of blankets!"

In Allahabad one day he said to Didi, "Kamala, it is very hot. I will take off my blanket and I want a shawl." She brought a thick one but he said, "No, this is too heavy. There is a shawl in that chest, bring that one."

Now in my college days I used to sometimes wear a shawl. A dear friend from the hills brought me a very fine shawl which was dove color and actually matched the kurta [a kind of tunic] that I wore. Babaji had never seen it, I rarely took it out of the chest, but he asked for that shawl and wore it that day. Later he gave it away.

When he gave away my clothes or blankets I didn't mind, but when he gave away my books I was not very happy. The books were very precious to me. When I was teaching in the university, I generally didn't borrow books from the library, I bought my own and I didn't like to lose them. So when Maharajji started distributing my books, it was hard. I thought at first I would hide them somewhere, but there was no way of saving them. One day Baba suddenly said, "You give away all my books and do not keep anything for me to read! You must keep my books." He took a book and wrote "Ram Ram Ram" in it and said, "This is my book and you must keep it." He did that to several and those books were kept on a shelf in his room. Afterwards I understood that he wanted me to read them. Those books about the saints and sages helped me to understand him.

While we were in Kainchi in 1972, I was alone with Babaji after he had taken his evening meal. He asked me who slept in one of the rooms in our house in Allahabad. I said, "Ma, Maushi Ma, Subodh and Vibouti."

"Who sleeps in Kamala's room?" he asked.

I said, "No one."

"Where does Ashoka sleep?"

Ashoka was staying at the house while we were away. I said she slept on the verandah. "Why does she not sleep in that room?"

"Because it is hot and therefore she sleeps outside."

"Accha, accha." The matter ended there.

The next morning a telegram came from my brother in Allahabad: "Dacoits broke open and ransacked the storeroom and took away jewels and ornaments." There was no question of leaving Baba to return to Allahabad.

Several days later Baba said, "Look at this fellow. There has been a theft in his house and they want him to go there, but he is completely indifferent about it." Later we came to know that the clothes and other things were not taken, but the ornaments of Didi and Ashoka were gone. Baba said, "Dada, they would not make charity, they would not make gifts. That is why the things have gone away."

People who saw Babaji in the ashram procuring supplies and urging their safekeeping could be forgiven for thinking that he was attached to these things. But they were misled. If he had been indifferent or very slack, everything would have easily vanished in no time. Once many stainless steel cups and plates came to the ashram, but within a few months most of them were gone. I said, "It is surprising that ashram supplies go away like that."

Babaji laughed, "Dada, here everything goes away as prasad. That is what has happened to your cups and plates."

The day of the main bhandara of the year, about five o'clock in the afternoon, a large number of people were still on the ashram premises waiting for Babaji to return to the ashram. We were standing in front of the temples when someone came running and told us a gang of young men had entered the ashram from the back side. They were knocking at every door, threatening people into vacating the rooms. Then we saw them—about fifteen young men—pounding against some closed doors and demanding the keys, which I held. They began shouting at me, "What do you people think about this ashram? Flatterers like you from the plains who surround Babaji have started to think this ashram belongs to you. You are fools. The ashram belongs to us—the ones who built it!" They threatened me and demanded the keys. One of the gentlemen standing in the group knew the troublemakers and was able to calm them down and persuade them to go away.

A short while later Babaji came rushing in, asking what the rumpus in the ashram was all about. Babaji began shouting at the people narrating the incident, saying, "They should have shot me and not insulted Dada like that!" Rushing out of the ashram, he got into the jeep. Reaching Bhumiadhar, he sat on the verandah by the road in the dark. The young men had travelled from Kainchi by truck, planning to set fire to the temple at Bhumiadhar. They began marching towards the temple, carrying burning torches in their hands. As they approached, Babaji jumped out towards them, roaring like a lion. They ran down the road, fearing for their lives. Babaji ran after them, driving them far away, and then returned to the temple. He was talking, as if to himself, "They wanted to make a fool of me. I knew what they were after and gave them a long rope." Later he laughed and told me, "They came to frighten me, but when I shouted at them it was enough to make them pee in their trousers!"

The next day everyone was talking of the incident. Babaji said it had been planned for a long time and that he knew the persons who were behind it. In the afternoon a man came, touched my feet, and began to apologize on behalf of his son, who had been one of the gang. I told him that I had not taken any offense, but he must go to Babaji and get his pardon. He said that he had seen Babaji first, who had sent him to me. This gentleman who was pleading for his son was the older brother of Haridas Baba.

When we reached Babaji's room, we saw him surrounded by the elderly relations of those involved in the rumpus. Some of them pleaded ignorance about the involvement of their children in the conspiracy, but Babaji refuted their arguments and exposed them all fully.

A few days later Haridas came from Hanumanghar. As Haridas was ill, Babaji went to his room to talk to him. Baba told me no one should come in, and the Mothers were actually locked in their rooms. I stood at the door. Babaji went on exposing the whole conspiracy and the people close to him who had been involved. His voice was raised to such a high pitch that many people became frightened at his loss of temper. Haridas had broken down and was crying the whole time.

Babaji was shouting: "Do you think that I am accumulating wealth and building up assets in ashrams and properties? Do you think I am going to be tied down by them? I shall burn Kainchi and go away!" Not only the people in the ashram, but those out on the road were actually trembling.

All this was because Haridas would not agree to leave Kainchi and this was a way of pushing him out. It was not that Maharajji had taken it to heart. It was just a shadow play. Later I said to him, "You cannot discharge anybody, you can only transfer!" That is what happened to Haridas. He wanted to build a small community of his own devotees. Therefore, Haridas was "transferred" and now, of course, has found his place. Baba did not make Haridas an orphan, or take revenge on him. He gave him what he wanted.

Those involved in the incident could see what Baba possessed, but did not see that the wealth or property did not possess him. It must have been painful for Baba to accumulate so many possessions, but it was a self-imposed pain. He suffered this because of his compassion—helping and assisting the helpless, doing good for others. He said, "Dada, I could have been a great saint, but I suffer from a serious handicap—too much compassion." It was that compassion that made him a prisoner.

When he left Kainchi for the last time he said, "Now I am leaving Central Jail." Even his blanket dropped from his body.

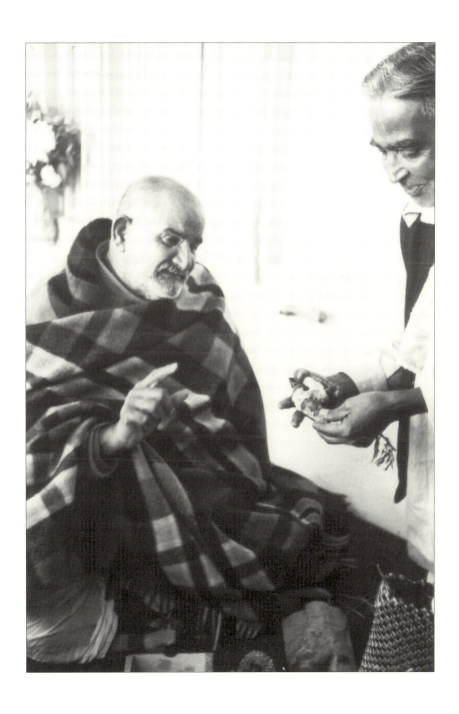

IX
ABUSES, JOKES, AND CARESSES

Babaji's ways were so peculiar. You could not imagine that such a saint could behave just like a child or like an ordinary person indulging in all kinds of jokes and mock fights, trying to provoke or embarrass people. Ram Dass and other Westerners used to come to me and complain that I did not translate everything Babaji said. The difficulty was that nobody could translate his abuses. He would go on saying, "Dada is an M.A., Dada is an M.A."

One day when he was abusing everyone much, I said to him, "You are also an M.A."

"How? How?"

"I am a Master of Arts; you are a Master of Abuses!"

He laughed, "Yes, yes, I go on abusing so much."

Many of the Western devotees got married while they were with Babaji; others were living together although not actually married. Among these were a fellow C. and an Australian girl, Uma. She was so nice and sweet. They eventually left India and she had a son. She sent a telegram to me in Vrindaban saying, "I have had a son. Please ask Baba to give him a name."

The next morning when I went to Babaji's room he said, "You had a telegram last night? What was it?" I told him Uma had a son and asked him to give a name. He said, "Wherefrom shall I get a name? All right, Dada, give him the name Khutka butka!" [Hocus-pocus!]

Siddhi Didi and Jivanti were there and they said, "What is this? Is it a name? Give the son of Uma a good name."

"You wretched women, wherefrom shall I get a good name? All the good names have been taken by ugly persons like you!" I just stayed quiet and waited for his fun to be over. After some time he said, "All right, give the name Ganesh. Uma [another name for Parvati] is the mother of Ganesh."

Later in the summer we were in Kainchi and again a telegram came for me from the States. It was delivered to me when I was with Baba. He immediately wanted to know, "What is it? What is it?" I told him who it was from. He said, "What do they want?" I told him they were going to have a baby and they wanted Baba to give a name. "What have you understood?" he asked me.

"What is there to understand? You have got to give a name."

"You are a fool!" he cried. "You don't understand. A name is given when a child is born. The child is not yet born, but they want a name. That is a trap for you—that you will extract a name from me and they will know if it will be a boy or a girl!" He told me not to send a reply. But later when he had retired to his room and we were alone together, he said, "You understand now?"

"Of course."

"Then you did not understand?"

"Of course I did not understand. I am a fool, how could I understand?"

"How did I understand?"

"Of course, Baba, you are very intelligent."

"And you?"
"I don't have brains."
"No, no, you also have brains."

I was one of the main targets for Babaji's abuse, but I took it as a manifestation of his affection. One year a certain family came from Lucknow to Kainchi and they were staying in the dharmashala outside the ashram gate. They said they would cook their own food, though of course they would take sweets or prasad from Babaji. They were given all the provisions they needed. The two teenagers would come and ask for this and that all the time—some special tea, or cups and saucers, or fruit.

One very busy day when many persons were there, Babaji went up to the back of the dharmashala and entered Kali Babu's room. He lay on the bed and talked through the window to people outside. I was standing near him by the door and one after another someone would come to me and ask for something—one of the cooks asked how many puris to cook, another came for instructions for purchases from Haldwani, and so on. Then one of those teenagers came asking for something and Maharajji said, "Look at Dada. What a fool he is. He is always running here and there, getting this and that for all these persons. I want to see the day that somebody comes and tells him, 'I want some cat piss,' wherefrom he will get the cat and how he will make it urinate!"

One day in 1973 three *Naga babas* came from Badrinath and they were given rooms in the outside dharmashala. They said they would need plenty of wood for their havan fire and various other provisions. "In Ayodhya fifty-four items of food are prepared for Ram. We have got a statue of Ram and we also offer him prasad and must prepare it."

One day, however, they wanted some ganja [marijuana]. This was a problem. I asked some of the ashram people who I knew were great smokers, but they pretended to have never heard of ganja. I did not know what was to be done, but a Westerner heard me asking and said, "Dada, I can give you some." So the ganja was given to them.

Babaji said, "Dada, it is good that you have done this. They live in the open and do not wear clothes, so the ganja will protect their bodies. They are accustomed to it, therefore they should have it." But there was a chance of having some entertainment from this. The next day when he was sitting outside with many persons around he said, "Look at Dada. Those sadhus have come and want so many things every day and he is running and getting it all for them. Tomorrow when they ask for a woman, let me see where he gets one."

Didi and I used to go to Kainchi in the first week of May when the university and Didi's college would be closed. We could stay till Didi's college would reopen in the middle of July. I could usually stay later because my classes were lectures and could be postponed. But we could both delay our departure until the end of July by getting a medical certificate for Didi's absence.

One year Didi had been promoted to a higher post and her medical certificate had to be countersigned by the highest medical man of the district. One morning I went with Purnanand and another devotee in the jeep to get the certificate in Bhowali and then to Nainital to get the certificate countersigned. We were much delayed in Bhowali and when we reached Nainital the Civil Surgeon said, "Where is the patient?"

I said, "The patient is in Kainchi."

He said, "No, no. If the patient does not come, I cannot countersign."

So we had to return. It was already late afternoon and Babaji was sitting outside on his cot. Our welcome was very hot. "Why are you so late? You have been spending the whole day talking and gossiping, you have got no sense of responsibility. Once you get out you forget everything! Have you got the certificate?"

Purnanand said, "Baba, we had a difficulty. The doctor said that without looking at the patient, he would not sign."

Maharajji shouted, "What a fool you are! Could you not get a woman in Nainital? What else is there in Nainital except women? You could have caught hold of your own daughter and taken her. Is anything written on the forehead that this is Kamala Mukerjee?"

In the afternoon at Kainchi when Maharajji would sit before the showers I could be a little free because there would be so many persons with him. I had many things to look after— the policeman at the gate who often felt neglected, the pujari who also needed someone to listen to his complaints, the Mothers asking for this and that. In the midst of it all, Khemua would come and we would try to take a cigarette. If someone would ask for me, Baba would say, "Dada is the president. He has no time for me. He is putting sweets in somebody's mouth, he is advising somebody, he has no time for me."

Once I heard him saying that and I said, "No, Baba, when you abuse, I am there."

People always got angry and annoyed because Babaji so frequently said, "Jao!" [Go!] to them. But there was usually some reason why he did not allow them to stay longer. It was better not to try and guess what the reason might be.

One winter in Allahabad he was giving darshan and the whole room was full. A certain officer in the Accountant General's office entered and took his seat in the rear. He had heard about Babaji from some of his fellow officers and was very curious to come. After a minute or so, Babaji said, "Jao!"

He replied, "No, Baba, I am not in a hurry. I shall sit here for some time."

"No! You must go." Babaji was insistent. The officer was unhappy. Everybody was looking at him, so he stood up reluctantly, wondering about this Baba. Then Babaji said, "You came on a cycle?"

"Yes."

"All right, return by the same way that you came." The man didn't understand, but he went.

The next day he returned and said, "Baba saved the life of my son. After I left, my small boy went out with his cycle and collided with a scooter. He was lying more or less unconscious there on the road, the same road. I picked him up and took him to a doctor."

In July 1972 we were in Kainchi and a Muslim gentleman came who was the general manager of the Roadways Bus Company in Bhowali. He was very much devoted to Baba and whenever he could take some time he would come. On that day he was sitting in Babaji's room and after about a half hour, Babaji said, "Jao!"

He said, "No, Baba, I am free and I have my own conveyance, so I shall stay."

After some time Babaji insisted, "You go."

Later someone returned from Bhowali and said there had been a serious accident—a bus coming from Haldwani had fallen into the flooded Bhimtal Lake. The general manager was needed to organize the rescue work. It was a great tragedy. The bus had been full of people returning from work and many schoolboys.

The next afternoon that gentleman came again. Maharajji took him to the small room we called his "office." Nobody but myself was allowed to come and both the doors were closed. The manager broke down, crying bitterly, "I can understand the old people dying, but the little children returning from school?"

Babaji tried to console him and was saying, "What is this life? These laws cannot be understood. But God's creation goes on like this—someone is coming, someone is going, new leaves are budding, old leaves are falling down." Babaji quoted from the scriptures, the Koran and the *Upanishads* for an hour. It was the only time I heard him speak from the scriptures in that way.

Another time in Bhumiadhar, Maharajji was sitting on the cot in his room and persons were coming from Nainital, Ranikhet and Almora. A retired major in the army and a retired civil surgeon were there and Babaji was abusing them in a way I had never heard before. They were actually trembling and all they wanted was to be allowed to go out of the room. Then he said, "Jao!" When they had gone away, he looked at me and smiled—I couldn't believe it was the same man. He said, "Dada, were you frightened?"

"No, Baba."

"It is also sometimes necessary to rebuke and abuse."

The explanation was that these persons had opened a nursing home for further treatment of patients who were discharged from the Bhowali tuberculosis sanitarium. It was a business proposition and they were taking the name of Neem Karoli Baba, saying that he would come to inaugurate it. They had not asked him, but had taken it for granted. He had been thrashing them about that.

After the storm was over, one of them came and said, "Baba, we have no hope that you will come."

He said, "Yes, yes, I will come." And actually Baba and myself went there. That was his way.

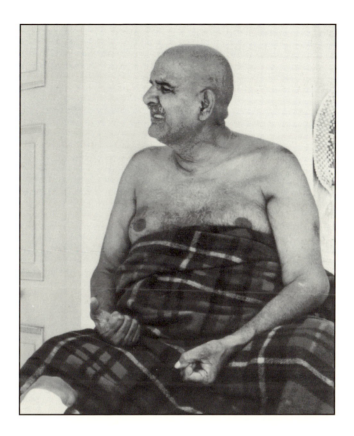

Mr. Sharma, an old devotee, was a taxi driver and frequently drove Maharajji from Kainchi or Bhumiadhar. One morning we got into his car at Bhumiadhar and drove down to the sanitarium near Gethia. Maharajji said, "Go and see if the doctor is there." When the doctor and I returned to the car, Maharajji got out and said, "I shall be hiding here. I don't want anybody to come." As Mr. Sharma was going away, Maharajji said to me, "Go and tell him that he should not talk to anybody."

I said, "I have told him."

"No, no. You go and tell him again. You do not know these paharis [mountain people]. They go to a hotel or tea shop and say, 'Do you know that Neem Karoli Baba has come? But you must not tell anybody!'" So I took some prasad to the driver and again told him not to talk to anyone.

Of course, soon people began coming and the doctor was very concerned that he would not have prasad for so many. We sent to Kainchi for puris, and while we were distributing them someone came and said, "The Mothers are standing outside under the tree and it is raining very heavily." They had walked from Bhumiadhar.

Maharajji shouted at me, "Where are you going?"

I said, "I am going to bring those persons."

He said, "Let them suffer, those badmash. I told them they should not come! Let them stand there!" But I brought them inside and they were given dry clothing. Who could imagine a saint talking the way he did?

The first time I went to Kainchi there was just one temple and a few rooms. Some construction was to be done and Babaji took me around and showed me where there would be so many bathhouses and so many toilets. After a few months, when the construction was completed, he said to me, "Dada, people have now started calling me 'Tatti Baba' [Latrine Baba]. That's very good." He had so many names and now he had a new one.

In the afternoon at Kainchi he would come and sit before the showers in a very jolly and relaxed mood. In 1973, he was supposed to be not keeping well, so he had to be properly wrapped. Siddhi Didi was very particular that he had to wear his pullover and blanket. I would try to put on his pullover, but sometimes it would be very difficult. One day it was getting dark and a little chilly, so I brought the pullover. As soon as I came, he said, "What is that?"

"Your pullover."

"I shall not wear it!"

So I said, "All right, don't wear it."

"Give it to me."

"Why should I give it to you if you are not going to wear it? I shall keep it with me." I kept it and people were looking. It was a very childlike sort of thing that he was doing.

Then he went on talking, but he kept looking at me suspiciously. I placed the pullover on his shoulders. He said, "What? This is what you do? You never obey me."

I said, "Let it remain, what difference does it make?"

Later a devotee said, "Oh, Dada, what fun we had. This was Bala Gopala's [Baby Krishna's] lila. How you make him do things!"

Once in the summer months in Kainchi, Babaji was wearing a tee shirt, a pullover and his blanket. When he entered his room, he dropped the blanket and I took off his pullover and tee shirt. The shirt was so wet with sweat that you could squeeze out drops of water. Siddhi Didi brought another tee shirt to put on him, but he pushed her away. "You wretched woman! I am dying of heat from these clothes and you are trying to put more on me!"

Balaram Das, one of the Westerners, used to take so many photographs and have them printed in Delhi. On the June fifteenth bandhara in 1973, Maharajji had Balaram take so many photos of the kitchen people, but allowed only a few of himself. When Balaram brought back the prints from Delhi, Babaji selected those of himself and put all the others of the kitchen workers in an envelope and said, "Give this to your Didi, she is very fond of pictures."

The Mas were waiting, eager for new photographs of Maharajji. "Let us see, let us see!" When I gave them the envelope, they cried, "What is the joke?"

I said, "How should I know what is there? It was just a closed envelope that he gave me."

Once I went to the bazaar near the Bihariji temple in Vrindaban to a small Gita Press shop. I found an illustrated Mahavir Hanuman, a short life sketch of Hanuman. I took all the copies that they had, about fifteen or twenty. When I brought them to the ashram, everybody wanted one. Maharajji actually snatched a copy from my hand. "You do not give me! You are distributing, but you do not give me!" He began reading it loudly. Balaram Das took some photos of him.

He could be very strict or very frightening, but if you were not taken in by the outer antics and if you tackled him properly, you could make him very soft and light. The June fifteenth bandhara in 1972 was coming and since it was the anniversary of the temple inauguration, a very attractive red dress was being made for Hanumanji's murti. I do not know how the idea came, but I thought there should be a red blanket for our Hanuman also. I asked Siddhi

Didi to have her sister or others bring one to Kainchi. She said, "Oh, Dada, we can get it, but he will not wear it."

I said, "Nevertheless, let us get it and keep it ready."

So the day came. Maharajji was out moving here and there and then returned to his room. I said to Balaram, who was there with his camera, "Be alert. There may be something."

When we were getting ready to come back out, I brought the red blanket to put on him. He said, "No! I don't like the red blanket. I won't wear it. I don't like it."

I cried, "You may not like it, but we like it. You must have it!"

"You are forcing me?"

"Yes, sometimes you have to be forced." I put the blanket on him. He went out and Balaram took those photos.

It would be such a problem for the barber to give him a shave. In Kainchi we had some old barbers who knew Babaji very well. While shaving would be going on, he and they would be talking to each other and they would actually be basking in his grace. It would take only about half an hour or so to do the shaving, but they would not be in a hurry and would stay the whole day. In Allahabad also an old barber would come and there was no problem. He understood Baba and was not in a hurry.

The problem came in Vrindaban when Babaji said, "I shall have a shave." We did not know any barber and Kishan Singh's son, Bapu, was asked to find one. He got a young man who ran a small shop in the bazaar. When that barber came, he was in a hurry because he had left his shop. The shaving was to be done in my room where there was an adjoining bathroom. The barber came and I went to get the hot water and other things. When I returned, I found that Babaji had taken the bedsheet from my bed and wrapped it around himself. Maharajji held the sheet tight and said, "You never give me this. Do not snatch it away."

I said, "I will not." So the shaving began. The greatest difficulty was that Baba would take the mirror in his hands and make faces in it.

The old and expert barbers knew how to deal with this, but the young man in a hurry was having trouble.

I said, "Baba, sit straight and let him shave you." But he kept moving and there was a cut. The barber was upset.

Maharajji said, "What is that? What is that?"

"Of course, it is a cut. This is what you have done. The poor fellow is embarrassed; he feels it is his fault. It is yours. You would not allow him peace to shave you."

Some alum was put on—it was only a small cut. The barber finished and went away. Babaji asked me, "Dada, will the hair grow here again?"

When Maharajji would go away from Allahabad, everyone would be asking where he had gone, but I would never disclose it. In 1972, when so many Westerners were there, they were keen to follow him if they could learn where he was going. Babaji said, "Dada, they will follow me if they know. They will go anywhere and everywhere. What will you do?"

I said, "Don't worry. I can manage."

"Tell me, tell me, what will you say?"

"Baba, now I have learned how to speak lies."

He laughed, "How, how, how?"

During the *Guru Purnima* celebration in 1972, he was giving all kinds of indulgences to the devotees, especially the Westerners. They washed his feet with a bucket of *panchamrita*, took sandalwood paste and wrote "Ram Ram" on his forehead. I was feeling a little unhappy, but Babaji kept saying, "Oh, Dada, let them do it, let them do it."

We were sitting before Babaji and someone said that if something was good it was all Babaji's grace and Babaji should be thanked. On the other hand, if something went wrong, the individual was responsible for it and should be blamed. I said, "I do not believe that. Why should Babaji take only the credit and I am to suffer the blame? No, no. If I do something good, he should take the credit. But he should also take the blame if something goes wrong."

Then Maharajji said, with tears in his eyes, "Why Dada said so? Why Dada said so?"

One day Baba and I were in his "office" in Kainchi. The doors and windows were bolted. He was leaning on his side and looking at something near the window. Outside the Westerners were singing

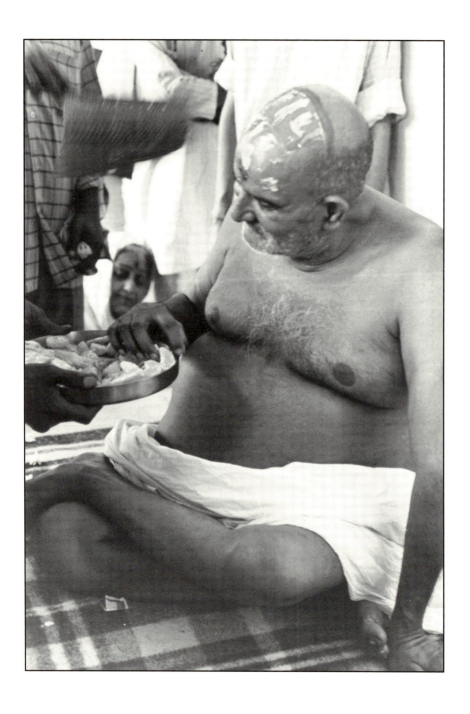

kirtan, but there seemed to be nothing else to take note of. Then he shouted, "Let me have some paper!" I didn't have paper, but I gave him a letter I had in my pocket. With very great care he picked up something on the letter and then gave it to me, saying, "Take it out."

As he was handing it to me, a fly flew away off the paper. Fly spray had been spread in the room and many flies had died, but some had only become unconscious. This one had been on the window sill. With great care he had picked it up and when it flew away he cried, "I caught it with such great effort and you allowed it to fly away!"

I also shouted, "It flew before it reached my hand. It was from your hand that it flew away!"

"Accha? I shall catch it again. I shall catch it again!"

That room—the "office"—was actually Babaji's temple. Babaji would be opening the window and closing it. Persons standing around would come rushing to see him or he would be yelling at them and then again close the window. Once a devotee said, "This is Biharaji's temple."[1] In that temple there is a curtain which is opened for Biharaji's darshan and then the curtain is closed. One cannot have continuous darshan of Biharaji, is it not that?

राम राम

---

[1] The Biharaji temple is a famous temple of Krishna in the town of Vrindaban, where the play of Krishna and the gopis took place. The murti of Krishna is hidden behind a golden curtain and only revealed during certain ceremonies each day.

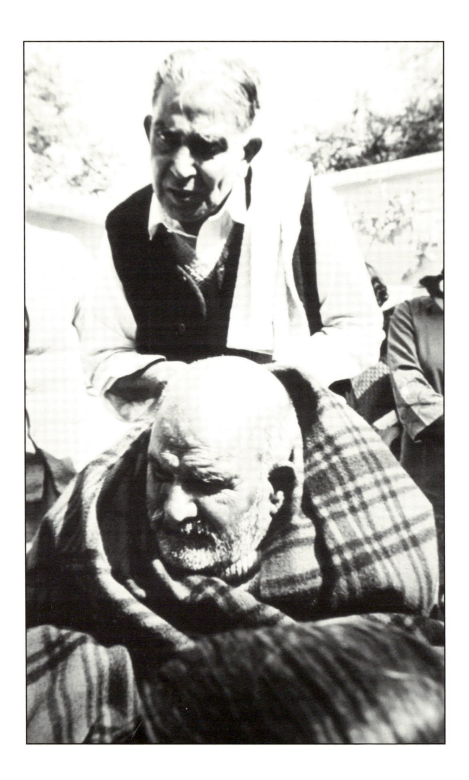

X
ILLNESS AND HEALING

There are so many stories of how Babaji healed people. My own brother Subodh, who lived with us, was very nearly blind. He was a good student and joined the education department as a temporary subinspector of schools. He was in that post for a long time, but he could not be confirmed until he submitted a medical certificate. Because of his poor eyesight he was afraid to go for a test, knowing that he would be rejected outright. He kept working on a temporary basis and the result was that he had foregone promotions and other benefits due him.

Now Babaji knew everything and it is certain that he must have been protecting Subodh all along. Once my auntie, who loved Subodh like a son, told Baba that she worried about him when he went out on tours of the villages and wanted him to stay home, safe and secure. Baba said, "Maushi Ma, there is nothing to fear, God moves with him."

However, the question of Subodh's confirmation remained. One day, Babaji said to him, "Tomorrow we shall go to the doctor in Pratapgarh and have your eyes tested." Subodh, of course, was nervous, but agreed since Babaji was taking him. The next day they drove to Pratapgarh and the doctor tested Subodh's eyesight. We do not know what trick Maharajji played, but Subodh received a certificate that his eyesight was quite all right. So he got his confirmation and continued in his job.

In the early days Babaji's photographs were few, and he himself did not want any publicity. When Didi received a picture it would be kept hidden in her puja room, and every morning and evening food would be offered to Maharajji's photo.

One day she found that there were spots on his body in the picture and Didi was very frightened at what this might mean. A few days later, my mother had an attack of smallpox and eruptions came out on her body. Babaji was not in Allahabad, but Siddhi Didi and others later told us that he had eruptions on his body at the same time and then they vanished. My mother also got cured very quickly.

In the early sixties, before we started going to Kainchi, I was teaching in the university and I was very fond of my reading and study. At night I sat for at least two or three hours at my desk and read. Then I would switch off the lamp in my study and pass through Babaji's room, stopping to bow at the left side of his cot. I would automatically put my hand on the leg of the cot. One night I felt a deep hole in the cot leg. Suddenly I thought, "I take this to be Babaji's leg. Am I mistaken?" I went on touching it, but I knew of no abscess or boil on his leg.

A few days later, Maharajji and K.C. Tewari arrived for an unscheduled visit. After we had all finished our food, I went into Babaji's room. He was on his bed and suddenly my eyes fell on his uncovered leg. I saw a deep wound, but said nothing. Babaji said "Kya? Kya?" [What? What?] But nothing registered; it didn't even occur to me to bandage it.

After Baba left, I remembered his wound and the hole in the leg of the cot. That made me crazy. I paced all night long. For many years I never talked about it to anyone, it was too painful and mysterious.

I have been told that long before the temple was built, Babaji came one night to a house in Bhumiadhar. An old gentleman was very ill and the family was just sitting, waiting for the last breath to pass. Babaji came and sat there and everyone began to hope that something might be done. It was very dark; there was no electric light at the time. In the darkness, two persons came, stood there and said, "Give us a carpet."

Babaji said, "Give it to them. Do not ask why they want it." So the carpet was given.

The men left carrying the carpet rolled up on their shoulders, crying, "Ram nam satya hai. Ram nam satya hai. . . ."[1] And that old man recovered.

One winter day in Allahabad a woman who came regularly said her husband was very ill. He had been suffering for some time with kidney trouble and uremia. Babaji told her he should be operated on during the winter months.

---

[1] See footnote page 41.

In the month of May that lady came to Kainchi. Her husband was then in very critical condition and there seemed no hope of survival, the *Ramayana* was even being read to him. When Babaji was told that the man had not had the operation, he cried, "Drive her away! Her husband is in critical condition and she comes here?" Babaji would not allow her to come near him.

She began to cry and said, "Dada, what is the matter? I came to Babaji for his blessing, what shall I do now?"

Baba said, "No, no, she will kill me also. Send her away!" And he actually gave her quite a few slaps. Later I learned that her husband had recovered and he lived for some time after that.

Sometimes it seemed that a cure was not possible. A judge of the Allahabad High Court was seriously ill and his son and daughter-in-law came to see Baba at our house. That lady cried bitterly and said, "Baba, my father-in-law is so very ill. You must do something."

Babaji just replied, "When your father-in-law is so very ill, why are you not at the hospital looking after him? Why are you coming and wasting your time here? Jao!"

Baba did not say that he would be all right. Nothing of the sort. He just rebuked her and sent her away. When she came again, he said, "No, no, you should be there with him. You can make him happy."

Then one day Babaji and I went to the hospital to see that man and the next day he died.

I have heard from many devotees how Babaji cured them or helped them to face their illnesses. He would not cure them by giving some ashes from his *dhuni*—he didn't have a dhuni—or by a pat on the head. He would tell them to see a doctor or take some medicine. The doctors to whom he sent people would say, "I only gave medicine, Baba gave the cure."

There was a devotee from Calcutta who was an amateur homeopath and gave medicine to people. Maharajji used to call him "my doctor." He would say, "I also sneeze sometimes, give me some of those pills." In this way he was blessing that man and encouraging him to continue to give medicine.

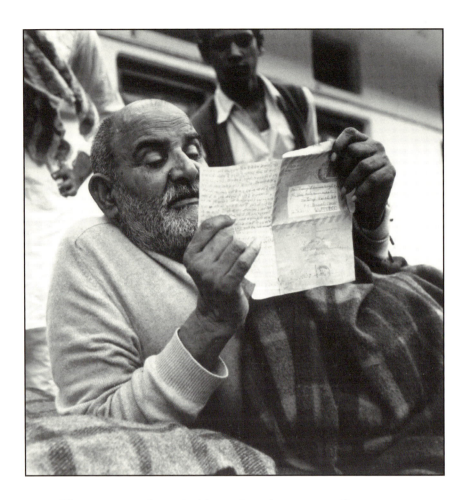

The man once brought his uncle, who was a sadhu, to see Maharajji. They sat for some time in the room and when they left, the uncle said, "How very fortunate that you have such a saint as your guru."

The devotee was rather curious, since his uncle had not spoken to Maharajji. "You wanted so much to talk to him, but you didn't say anything."

The uncle answered, "Whatever I had to know, he communicated."

One day Maharajji came to Allahabad after having been in Lucknow and he seemed to be a little disturbed. I went with him to his room and he said, "Dada, your friend is very ill."

I understood that he was referring to Sang, who was in the hospital in Lucknow. I asked, "Baba, thik ho jayengi?" [Will he be all right?]

After a moment he answered, "I do not know." I knew then that the end was near.

I said to him, "God can cure him."

"God can do everything," was his answer.

Babaji later went to see Sang. In the hospital room were Sang's wife and children and a few friends. Maharajji's chair was drawn near Sang's bed. Each and every one had so much on their minds and hearts. Sang, of course, was not talking. He was just bending down, catching hold of Babaji's feet. A few tears fell on Maharajji's feet. Babaji said, "If you cry, I will go away."

Sang replied, "Baba, these are not tears of pain or parting. These are tears of joy and fulfillment. You are here. I have got everything."

One morning when Babaji was staying in Bhumiadhar I went to his room and found a number of the Mothers there. They were very much disturbed and said, "Dada, since last night Babaji is having great pain in his knee."

I came to him, "What's the matter?"

"Oh, Dada, there is very much pain."

I said, "Why are you unnecessarily teasing these persons? You don't have any pain."

He said, "No, Dada, there is very much pain." So I asked what was to be done. "Get me that medicine, that mocha [sprain] wallah medicine—the medicine with the moustache!"

I could not understand what he meant—could a medicine be made out of moustache? He insisted on having it, so I went to Bhowali, a very small town nearby, to see if there was any such medicine. I had given up searching and was waiting for the bus near a small stationery stand. The owner knew me well and began talking to me. He sold all kinds of things: books, papers, pens and pencils. When I was looking in the case I saw a carton with the picture of a hefty person who had a big moustache—it was Sloan's Liniment. I purchased it and a packet of cotton and brought them back to Bhumiadhar.

"You have brought that medicine?"

"Yes, of course."

"And what is this?"

"It is cotton. After the massage, the knee has to be wrapped with cotton."

"Oh no, Dada, that is not necessary! Only a little massage of that medicine will do, that is enough."

I said, "No, you have been creating problems for these persons and making them worry. Now you must have your knee wrapped."

He said, "No, just put a little liniment." That was done and the knee was all right.

An old devotee, Kali Babu, came often to Kainchi ashram. He, too, had pain in his knees and joints and he used to put on an elastic bandage. When he came, Babaji asked, "What is that? What are you wearing?"

"Babaji, it is a knee bandage, and I wear it when I have pain. It gives much relief."

"Can you get one for me? I also sometimes get a knee pain." So he got it and Babaji actually sometimes would put it on in his room, but he would never come outside with it on.

Maharajji had serious kidney trouble at Vrindaban at a time when none of the Mothers were there. Many doctors were called who gave medicine, but with no relief. After three days, Babaji came to be all right. Everyone was very disturbed. I heard about it when I came to Vrindaban a month later and asked Babaji about it.

"One day I had something wrong with my urine. It was coming too often. These persons got upset and called a doctor. He came and examined me. He said, 'The tube has burst.' I said, 'My tube has burst, but your tube is all right. Enjoy your good tube.' After that a bigger doctor came from Delhi. He said, 'The urinary bladder has burst.' I said, 'Let your bladder be broken, my bladder is all right!'"

This is how he was narrating the story with his inimitable gestures and postures. Then he said, "I told these people, 'Let these doctors go, don't get any more of them. They do not know anything. They are giving wrong advice and frightening you.' Then I went to my devotee, that great doctor in Agra, and he

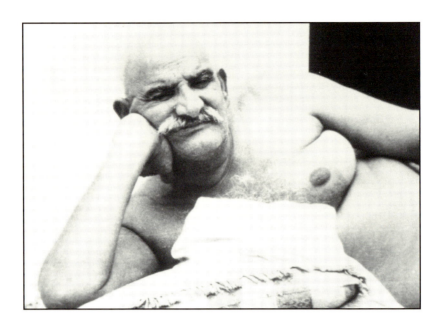

said, 'Babaji, there is nothing, only that you caught cold,' and he gave me a tablet. I was all right."

The next year the Mothers said to me, "Dada, Babaji had that trouble with his urine. Something must be done to test it. Also, he is not interested in taking his food." He had stopped eating sweets altogether. So they thought there should be a test of his urine. Of course it had to be done in secret.

One morning the urine was collected and I took it to a doctor's clinic in Vrindaban. That doctor was known to us and I waited for him for some time, but he did not come. His father said to leave the sample and it would be tested when the doctor came and the report sent to us. When I returned to the ashram, Babaji asked, "You got the report?"

I said no, and explained the situation. He shouted at me, "What a fool you are! They will mix up the sample and send a report that is wrong. This is how they go on with their business. They will make a complicated report and prescribe a lot of medicines and injections. Go and get it and throw it away. Tell them I don't want any test." I did that, but, of course, the matter did not end there.

Three or four days later, the Mothers again said I should take a sample to the Ramakrishna Hospital nearby. This time it had to be done in my own name. When I got the report it said everything was all right. When I brought it, Baba said, "You have got it?" He actually threw that report. "You people are unnecessarily bothering me. Nothing is there." So that is the kind of thing that was going on.

In 1972 Babaji once complained that there was something wrong with his heart. It was painful and he could not sleep at night. Of course, there was no question of his sleep—he would be awake all night whether ill or not. Someone suggested that he be taken to Dr. Joshi, the Civil Surgeon, at Nainital. Babaji just looked at me and said, "Joshi is coming this morning." He was a devotee and sometimes came to Kainchi and had actually said he would be coming on that day.

When Dr. Joshi heard the story, he said Maharajji should come to have a test at Ramsay Hospital in Nainital. The next day the devotees took Babaji to the clinic where the electrocardiogram machine was kept. All the talk was about the machine, where it was made, how it was made, and Babaji wanted to see how it worked. There was no talk of disease or illness. The test was made and nothing was wrong.

Before Maharajji took his *mahasamadhi* there was such a drama created in Kainchi. For two days all the devotees were confused and upset because it seemed that Babaji had had a heart attack, but the doctor had come and said he was all right. On the ninth of September when Babaji said he would leave, Inder at first refused to take him to the train station because Baba had not been well. However, Babaji insisted and it was done. On the day that he took his *samadhi*, he visited his devotee in Agra, the doctor, who examined him and found everything—heart, pulse, everything—perfect. How is it to be explained?

XI

LAST DAYS

The following segment, taken from *Miracle of Love*, pp. 371-373, is offered as an introduction to this chapter, for those who are not already familiar with the story.

The Great Escape

What was to be Maharajji's final day at Kainchi was spent in darshan, kirtan, and prayers. Both Indian and Western devotees were gathered. Maharajji was asking after everyone at the temple and elsewhere. Twice he put one of his Indian devotees into samadhi and brought him out of it by throwing his blanket over the man's head. At one point he said to those gathered, "He is your guru. He is young and I am old. He will live and I will die!" Everyone laughed. He then had the Westerners sing to Hanuman. There were tears in his eyes. The Indian women did arti before him, and one and all received a tilak upon the forehead.

Then he went to bathe and eat and hinted that he was leaving for four or five days. When he came out of his room he went to the temple and paused before the murti of Hanuman, holding his hands together in pranam silently for two or three minutes. Again he stopped and honored each of the murtis at the temple in turn. While crossing the bridge out of the temple compound he met an old devotee who was a photographer. Maharajji gave him an old photo and told him to copy it and distribute it freely. He instructed that the daily feeding be stopped and the Mothers taken to Nainital. Then he said softly, "Today, I am released from Central Jail forever." As he approached the car that was to take him to the station, the blanket slipped from his shoulders to the ground. A devotee tried to put it back on, but Maharajji said, "Leave it. One should be attached to nothing." Others folded it and placed it in the car.

Just at the moment when he sat in the car, an old woman arrived from the nearby village of Bhowali. Maharajji said, "Ma, I've been waiting for you." He touched her on the head and said, "I'm going." He was gay and full of humor.

The driver of the car was another old and trusted devotee. He reports that during the ride to the railway station, he became aware that Maharajji's feet had become extremely big. "I was afraid," he said.

Maharajji kept saying to him, "What is destiny? What is going to happen? Tomorrow we don't even know." They got to the station early for the train, so they sat in the car for two hours. Maharajji pointed out a beautiful rainbow and said, "Look at that natural beauty. How beautiful is God's creation, man can never make anything so beautiful."

Tickets had been purchased to Agra for him and for Ravi, a young devotee. On the train Maharajji did not close his eyes all night, and kept waking the devotee and saying, "I'm not tired, talk with me." Ravi asked him to drink the milk which the Mothers had sent in a thermos, but the milk had turned bad. "Throw it out," Maharajji said, "Throw the thermos out, too." Ravi didn't want to, but Maharajji did so himself, saying, "Throw it out. I will not need it anymore." He spoke of many things and many people through the night. He said, "I've come on earth only for the spreading of dharma."

When they reached Agra, Maharajji jumped from the train while Ravi trailed behind with the baggage. Instead of following the platform, Maharajji jumped from it easily, crossing six sets of tracks and jumping up on the main platform. Ravi caught up with him at the ticket-taker who had stopped Maharajji for his ticket. Then Maharajji bargained with various rickshaw drivers: one wanted three rupees (about thirty cents), which Maharajji argued was too much. Finally a price was fixed and they set out, only Maharajji knowing the way. En route, Maharajji pointed out a house and said, "Their son has gone to America and the family feels very sad. Sons don't serve their fathers any more." When they arrived at the house, he told Ravi to give to the rickshaw driver the milk bucket filled with Ganga water that Maharajji always carried with him. Again he said, "Have no attachment for anything."

Except for one hour when Maharajji went to see a heart specialist (he had complained of pains in his chest), he remained at S's house *from 6:00 a.m. to 9:00 p.m. that evening. The specialist said that Maharajji's heart was fine and that he just needed rest. At 9:00 p.m. he left for the station to meet the train that would take him back up to the foot of the mountains at Kathgodam. He was accompanied by young Ravi and another devotee, D. After some time he told Ravi to go and sit in the next compartment. Ravi went there but was thought to be a thief by the occupants, who yanked the chain and had the train stopped. Ravi was taken up and placed in the police van that was a part of the train. Ravi persuaded the police to ask Maharajji at the next station if Ravi was with him. Maharajji was very loving to Ravi and said, "We'll get off at Mathura and I'll make a call to the DIG [Deputy Inspector General] and set things straight." At Mathura, not far from Agra, they got off the train. Some people bowed to him. He then sat down on the steps of the station after leaning against the outdoor latrine. D went to get a taxi, while R waited with Maharajji.*

Maharajji then lay on the steps and began convulsing. His eyes were closed and his body was cold and sweating. D fed him some pills and Maharajji said, "Turn off the lights." He asked for water and to be taken to nearby Vrindaban. He was carried by stretcher to the taxi and laid across the back seat. During the ride to Vrindaban, Maharajji seemed unconscious for most of the way, though now and then he mumbled things they could not understand. They took him to the emergency room at the hospital. In the hospital the doctor gave him injections and placed an oxygen mask over his face. The hospital staff said that he was in a diabetic coma but that his pulse was fine. Maharajji roused and pulled the oxygen mask off his face and the blood pressure measuring band from his arm, saying, "Bekar! [Useless]" Maharajji asked for Ganga water. As there was none, they brought him regular water. He then repeated several times, "Jaya Jagadish Hare" [Hail to the Lord of the Universe], each time in a lower pitch. His face became very peaceful, all signs of pain disappeared. He was dead. No one at the hospital had recognized him. The hospital staff left the room. Ravi and D carried Maharajji out and placed the body in a taxi and took it to the Hanuman temple. (It was about 1:15 on the morning of September 11.)

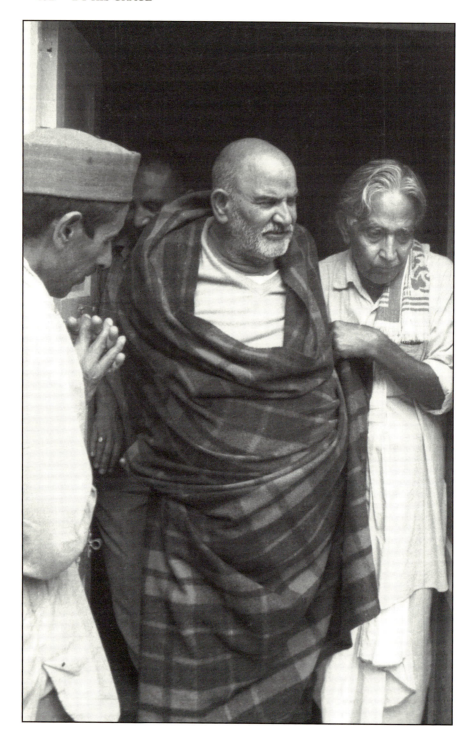

After 1970 I saw how very restless Babaji had become, that he just wanted to go away. He said, "Dada, I shall not have any more temples. It is very easy to build a temple, but so very difficult to run it."

Since I had met him he had been talking constantly of building new temples and dharmashalas here and there—at Jagganath Puri, Badrinath, Chitrakut, Benares, Gaya, Allahabad. Suddenly it all changed. Now he began saying, "Dada, what is attachment for a saint? I shall run away." This he would repeat many times a day, but I was not to tell anyone. I knew that it was with very great effort that he was staying. He quoted, "'The yogi who is always on the move and the water that is always moving, no sediment, no impurity can stick to them.' I used to move so much, I used to move so much . . . I shall move again, I shall move again."

Siddhi Didi also suspected something and when I was at Kainchi we would compare notes every day. She would say, "Dada, what is going to happen?" We tried our utmost to guard him in every possible way, but we could not speak of it to anyone else. We knew that he had no attachment for the ashram or for anybody. He was there and we were with him, that was all. It was like a rented house: while we are there it is so very dear to us, but when we leave it, we do not look back. Now when he said he would go away, I thought he would just be leaving the ashram as he had left other places. I didn't suspect that he would leave his body. After he took his samadhi, Rajuda's mother, who was a very great devotee, accused me of knowing that Maharajji was going to take samadhi. She would not believe that I did not know.

In Kainchi one day he was in his room resting after taking his food when suddenly he came out with just a tee shirt and dhoti on, no blanket. He hurriedly caught hold of my hand, saying, "Let's go!" We went out of the ashram and down the road. He asked, "Dada, have you been to Badrinath?" I said no. "We shall hire a taxi for six hundred rupees and go to Kedarnath and Badrinath. That is the land of the gods, the rishis and the great sages. I shall remain there, but you will return."

When I came to Kainchi in May of 1972, Baba told me, "Dada, I am not coming anymore to Allahabad. I have been coming there continuously for the last fourteen years. If one comes much and stays much, attachment comes."

People from Allahabad who were sitting there were furious with me because I answered, "Then don't come."

One morning Maharajji was with the Mothers in his room after taking his bath. Something had been said and Siddhi Didi began to cry very bitterly. Maharajji shouted for me and said, "Dada, you take your Didi from here, otherwise I will go away!" They had been

talking and he had said, "Am I indebted to anybody? Have I any attachment for anybody? Do you think that I am bound and tied? I shall leave Siddhi also!" This he went on shouting.

He began to have little consciousness of his body or his surroundings. Formerly in the morning he would do his toilet, clean his mouth, take a little milk tea and some fried gram flour. After that he would be very anxious to come out of his room. The Mothers would be doing arti to him and he would not want to wait for them to finish. But in the latter days he was not interested or willing to come out; he would just sit, talking and joking with the Mothers. One day he was talking about Draupadi's plan to charter a plane to take Maharajji and the Mothers and some devotees to America. He said to me, "Believe me, the Mothers have already prepared their frocks!" They all laughed so much.

Now it would be eight-thirty in the morning and the people would be waiting outside the room on the verandah. With difficulty I would bring him out, as if he had to go through a routine of work. He would sit and talk, but he did not have the old interest and energy.

In the afternoon he would sit in the back of the ashram. Sometimes I would take him to urinate. Formerly, I would just wait nearby; now I had to sit along with him and catch hold of his blanket and his dhoti. One day I had gone to do some work and when I returned he jumped up and caught my hand and began running. Mr. Barman said, "Maharaj, as soon as Dada comes, you go away?"

Maharajji responded, "Dada forgets that I have to urinate."

One day coming from the latrine he dropped his dhoti completely. Siddhi Didi sent for a *langoti* and he came to the room and just lay on the bed to be dressed like a baby. He said, "Ma, I shall become a child again, I shall become a child again."

We would give him his food and he would just take the spoon and tap on the plate or move the food around. There was no question of eating. If we wanted him to eat, we had to take the spoon and put food in his mouth.

He also began asking for old devotees to be called, persons who had not been allowed to come to the ashram in many years. One of these was Thakur Jaidev Singh, who had met Babaji in 1934 but had not seen him since then. Even so, his love and devotion were so intense that when he was called, he came. Babaji was sitting before the showers and saw Thakur come through the inner gate. He was a very tall, old man and came with his son and grandson, who were holding him on either side. Babaji told me, "Go and help him."

But when I went and tried to catch hold of his arm, he said, "I

have come to the person from whom all help comes. No other help is needed here."

At the June fifteenth bhandara in Kainchi in 1973 there was a record number of people. Everyone was asking me to bring Babaji out, but he sat in his room, unwilling to move. "No, Dada, let me rest, let me rest. I don't want to go." The ceremonies could not begin because he would not come out. After I tried twice and he would not come, the band began playing.

Later I went to try again to bring him and found him alone singing "Shri Ram, Jai Ram," dancing with his dhoti falling down. I had to catch hold of his dhoti and stand there. I had never seen him like that, with so little body consciousness. It was as if he had already left and only the body was there.

In 1972 and 1973 he began collecting many provisions for the Kainchi ashram—so many bags of wheat, so many bags of sugar. In 1973 seventeen truckloads of firewood were brought and lumbermen from Bhowali came to cut it. He would ask, "How much is left? Will it last until October? There will be much need for firewood then."

As it came to be, Maharajji took his samadhi in Vrindaban and therefore the cremation and ceremonies were done there. The mountain people had wanted his body brought to Kainchi, but when Pagal Baba said it must be done in Vrindaban, they left and decided to have their own bhandara. When I came on the third day, I learned of the quarrel. It was very painful to see that the cremation fire was still burning and already there was a quarrel between Vrindaban and Kainchi. The Kainchi bhandara was to be the day before the Vrindaban one and we went there. But because we did not want to create more of a split, we and the Mothers left Kainchi on the day of that bhandara and went to Vrindaban for the main ceremony. Although there was very little money at Kainchi, that bhandara came from what Maharajji had stored up. He knew all that was to happen.

For myself, it had been the thirteenth of August when we left Kainchi, a month before his samadhi. Didi's college had already opened, my university was opening soon. We came to see Maharajji in his room before we went. He said, "You are going? When will you come again?"

"Baba, whenever you want me to come, I shall come."

He only said, "Accha." Later Siddhi Didi said that after we had gone he kept saying, "Dada has gone away, Dada has gone away, but the work will go on. When I go away, the work will go on."

He made everything clear, but no one understood. Although there was deception, he was actually telling everything. On the day that he left Kainchi, he was asked, "Why must you go today?" His answer was, "I have got a date tomorrow." When they asked, "When shall we come?" he said, "Come on Tuesday."[1]

Maharajji took his samadhi. When we think of it, we may feel that perhaps everything has ended. But in my heart of hearts I have never felt that it was the end. I felt it was just a storm that had come and torn away some branches and leaves here and there, but the garden continued.

Even during the last days in his body, it seems he was showing his grace and saving me from a lot of unhappy dramas that would have been very difficult for me to survive. After he took his samadhi in Vrindaban, messages were sent by phone to those who had connections. Because we had no telephone, an express telegram was sent to us. The telegram arrived the next day after noon, when I was in the university. When I returned from the university, I took tea in my room. Then my mother said, "There is a telegram for you."

I came out and read the telegram, which was from Ravi Khanna: "Maharajji has taken his samadhi, come immediately." I could not believe it. I was very much upset. When Didi returned from her college, she also read it and it was difficult for her to believe. She went to the neighbor's house and telephoned to the Barmans in Delhi. Mrs. Barman said that it was true and that Mr. Barman had gone to Vrindaban in the morning.

We informed other devotees in Allahabad and it was decided that we would leave by the first available train. The train was at eleven o'clock that night and Rajuda, Pantji, Mukund, Kutul, Didi and I all went on it. We reached Mathura the next day in late morning. On the way to Vrindaban we passed two buses returning to Nainital with devotees who had come from there.

When we reached Vrindaban it was the third day after the mahasamadhi and there was a large crowd. The fire was still smouldering. The first person who came to us was Vishwambar. He said, "Oh, Dada, you are so very late. We were waiting for you until yesterday afternoon, but when you did not come we had to light the fire."

[1] On the following Tuesday, September 11, 1973, Maharajji left his body in Vrindaban. Devotees were contacted on that day to come for the cremation.

On hearing this, of course, tears came to my eyes. I saw those very ugly pictures that were being displayed: a photographer had taken so many of Maharajji's body and they were being sold. It was very shocking, but I thought, "Baba, you have been so very gracious and compassionate all through and even in the last moments you did not forget me. Had I been here, I should have been asked to put a fire stick to the funeral pyre. You have saved me from it."

Nobody understood my tears. They thought I was crying in sorrow at his parting. They said, "Dada, you should not cry." How could I explain?

The next person that spoke to me was Mr. Mehrotra. He said, "Dada, you did not tell us that Maharajji was a heart patient."

I actually lost my temper and shouted, "What are you talking about? What disease, what illness did he not have? From the hair on his head to his toenails, each part and cell of his body was full of disease. He had taken my illness, he had taken your illness, he had taken from all of us. That is why we are enjoying our good life—he has paid for it."

It was so striking that the place where he was cremated was in the ashram courtyard where a row of trees had been planted a year or so before. When those trees were being planted in a line from the front of the courtyard up to the dharmashala in the back, Baba told me, "Dada, leave a gap in the middle and don't plant any trees there." Then when I saw where the fire was smouldering, I knew that he had prepared the place and that people were unnecessarily fighting among themselves that he should be cremated somewhere else. He knew much in advance what drama, what trick he was to play, and prepared the stage. I was feeling helpless because the parting was certainly very painful. One could not get over the shock so very easily. However I might argue and console that he is not gone, still I was a human being and could not take it with such a stout heart, as I sometimes pretended to do. I was very much upset.

Before we were to leave the next day, it was decided that the ashes and flowers would be collected to be immersed in a number of places. Some would go to the Ganges in Hardwar, some to the sangam at Allahabad, and other places. The ashes for Allahabad were to be brought to our house and immersed by us. Mukund, Rajuda, and others brought the urn there and it was kept in Babaji's room.

Devotees from Delhi, Lucknow and other places had asked us to wait until Sunday, when they could come and join in the ceremony. So for three days the urn was kept in the room and every evening the Hanuman Chaleesa was sung.

On Sunday the urn was to be taken for immersion. On Saturday night, when the kirtan was over, the flowers were being collected from his bed and the bed cover was to be removed. The idea came to me that his bed could not be empty, as if everything had ended. How could his bed be empty when he had said, "I am always here"?

The idea came that there should be a picture, and the one that was at hand was a picture of his feet that was taken by Balaram. After all, a guru's feet are the same thing as the guru himself, rather more precious than the guru's body. The photograph needed a frame, but it was eight o'clock at night so the question was how to get one. I asked my nephew Vibouti to go to the Civil Lines market and buy a frame. Everyone said, "No, it is eight o'clock at night, the shop will be closed." But I insisted that he go and try. The photographers knew me very well and they lived in the adjoining area; he could take my name and get it. Vibouti returned so very happy with the frame and I was also overjoyed. The framed photograph was put on Maharajji's bed.

The next day such a large number of persons came, not only from Allahabad, but elsewhere also. The urn was taken in a procession to the sangam. It was the middle of September and the flood waters of the Ganges had not yet fully subsided, so large barges were engaged to take us to a sand bar in the middle of the river. In one barge the priest, Triveni Prasad, along with Mukund, Rajuda, myself, Didi, Mr. Ojha, Pantji, and many others took the urn.

Ceremonies had to be performed and there was no question of my doing them because I knew nothing about it. Mukund did them. Then came the offering of the rice bowl and they said I was to do it. Generally, the eldest son does it; but a saint is not supposed to have a son and therefore the favorite disciple does it. At first I refused to do it, but they insisted and finally I had to get down into the water. The current of the river was so strong that some persons had to hold onto me while I recited the mantras and made the offering. I had been more or less in a trance or semiconscious state all this time, but at that point I woke up and tears came in my eyes. I thought,

"You have filled both my hands with all I desired, all the sweet and good things, and look what I am offering to you."

Some days later Didi and I went to Kainchi for the bhandara that was to be held there on the day before the bhandara in Vrindaban. I said to Siddhi Didi that we had to go to Vrindaban for that bhandara, in order not to create more bad feelings. So we and the Mothers left Kainchi just after the bhandara started and took a taxi to get the train at Haldwani. We reached Vrindaban the next day and the bhandara was going on. It was a very busy day, full of activity, with no time to sit or talk or reflect.

Later in the day more Kainchi persons came—Inder, Jiban and others. They said that after we had left, some people came with constables wanting to capture the ashram. They had said Babaji had left the ashram without an heir and since it was full of precious metals and jewelry it should be taken into government custody, otherwise it would be looted. It was a big problem for the devotees. Shankar Dayal Sharma, a devotee of Babaji who held a high position in the government, had come to Vrindaban to the bhandara and I told him of the difficulty. He said, "Let us go to Delhi and take care of the matter." We reached his house that night where he telephoned the Home Minister. The Governor of Uttar Pradesh was contacted and ultimately a trust was set up to be responsible for the ashram. The trust started functioning in 1975 and I was connected to that until I resigned in 1976.

XII

AFTERWARD

Nowadays people come to me and say, "Dada, shall we see him again in his body?"
I say, "Look here, you may be having his darshan, but if I see him again I will say, 'Do not come in that body anymore!' He carried us in his arms for twenty years and what did we learn? Now if he would give a glimpse of that body, what would that do? What are we missing simply because he is not in a body? He has lived for us, he has given everything to us. I have no need to see that body again."

There are stories of Maharajji being seen here and there. I do not take them seriously, but perhaps these people are very keen to see him in that form and he comes. But what body he may be in, I do not know. That he is alive, of course, that I do know. I have never said that he is not alive. Otherwise how do we feel so strongly that he is here with us? How are so many persons still coming to him? But for those who have known him for twenty or thirty years, did not take much interest, and now suddenly want to see that body, what is the use of that?

People in India have a very great regard for the Ganges River. They come from distant places to take a bath in the Ganges, but bathing in the river does not mean that it purifies them. The tortoise goes on living in the Ganges for its whole life! If you have not the right kind of devotion, you can take a bath for your whole life and it will not change you. Is it not that?

Deoria Baba, himself a great saint, comes to Allahabad every year during the Magh Mela or the Kumbha Mela. A few years back he was here and some of his devotees who are well-known to us came to our house for satsang. They said that the night before they had been sitting around Deoria on the sand and someone came who said that he used to go to Neem Karoli Baba, but he is not there anymore, so he cannot go. Deoria Baba actually shouted at him, "What are you saying? Can such a saint go anywhere? He has done such kinds of tricks many times before! He is alive, and he always will be alive!"

It has also been told that Deoria Baba said that if persons had not been trying to keep Maharajji in the ashram and sitting around him to create a barrier or enclosure, he might have stayed longer here. Two things are very interesting: that he wanted to go away and that he was never reconciled to this kind of life of the ashram. He was essentially a tramp, a free spirit. There is no record of how many years he was wandering here and there, just bits of stories that we have got of how he was seen in so many places. It was only in the latter part of his life that all these ashrams were created. Even then he would not be in the ashram all the time. He would go out to many places—to Chitrakut, Amarkantak, Jagganath.

The third thing was said by that saint who came to our house and entered Babaji's room and saw his picture. He explained that Babaji was in sahaja samadhi, the samadhi that comes automatically, spontaneously. He said, "Look, the body is there, but don't you see that he is not in the body?" I myself had seen that. In the beginning, I used to get a little annoyed that he was in that kind of samadhi, especially when people would come to touch his feet, or sit close to him, or have prasad. But afterwards I became reconciled.

People asked me so often, "Why does Babaji go on covering himself with a blanket?" Not only would he wear a blanket in the winter when it was cold, but also in the hottest summer months. I used to say that there were two blankets: one blanket covered his physical body, that we all knew. It was not indispensable; it could be thrown off. Some miracles were no doubt done through it: he would be taking something out from under it, sometimes the blanket would be very heavy, sometimes it would be light, and there was the smell of a baby in it. But there was another blanket that was inside. He was covering all his sadhana, all his *siddhis,* all his achievements, all his plans and programs. Why was he hiding all this? Perhaps it was for our protection, perhaps to save himself from crowds of followers. We cannot know.

When Babaji said, "You stay at home," I did not know what it meant. Now I understand. I am actually within those four walls most of the time. When he said to me, "Dada, what is family life for you? Become entirely my own," I said, "Hah, Baba, thik hai." [Yes, Baba, that's fine.] When he said, "Become entirely mine," I did not know what it meant and said yes. Now I see that my thoughts, my ideas, my vision, everything is concerned with him, nothing other than him.

Sahaja samadhi photo referred to by Deoria Baba.

XIII

FLOWERS

On October 12, 1974, a holiday, I went out to a bookshop about twelve o'clock. My mother, my auntie, my brother, all were sitting on the porch. About one o'clock I returned and went through Babaji's room to go to my own. I found that the picture of Maharajji's feet that was always kept on his bed since his mahasamadhi had changed direction. It had been facing south, now it was turned to the east. The odd thing was that the picture had been turned, but the line of flowers had not been disturbed. There was also a copy of the Hanuman Chaleesa there that Maharajji used to keep under his pillow. When children came, he would take it out and say, "Read from this." That Hanuman Chaleesa had been taken out from under the pillow and placed in front of the picture.

Usually I put gardenia flowers before the picture, but that day for some reason I had put a saffron-colored flower from a creeper in the garden. It had no smell, so it was not normally used, but we called it "Hanuman's flower." That flower was put on top of the Hanuman Chaleesa.

I asked, "Who has turned this?" They said, "We have been sitting here the whole time, nobody has come, so no one could have turned it."

When other persons came to hear of this, they said, "Maharajji has revealed himself. He actually placed the Hanuman Chaleesa there and put the flower on it!" Now October 12th is an important day. We have a Sundarakand reading and bandhara each year on that date.

From then on I put flowers on the bed a little more systematically. After some time a sadhu came and the question came up about why the direction of the photograph had been changed. He said, "You do not know? He was facing south. South is the gate of death, people go by the south gate. He was showing you, 'Do you think that I am dead?' and therefore changed the direction."

I went on placing the flowers and the idea came, "Let me write 'Ram Ram' on the Hanuman Chaleesa," and with small flowers or leaves I began doing that. After some time, the idea came that I should also make a symbol of Babaji's feet. That is how the flower arrangements started. In the beginning, when it was changing almost every day, the devotees wanted some sketches to be done. At first I said no, but they kept asking and Didi said she would do the sketches.

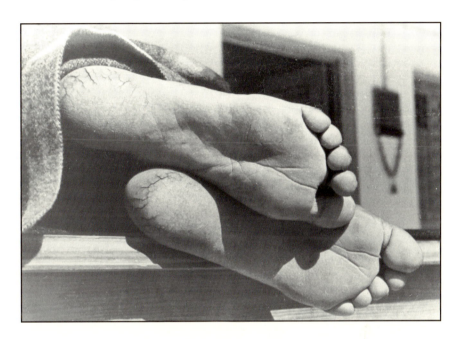

Now there is no escape from it; we have to do it. It takes three hours or more, but every day it is done. I do not know what or why it is, but we must do it, that's all. Perhaps it is to keep us occupied.

राम राम

XIV

THE SAINTS AND THE SAGES

The following is excerpted from a talk given by Dada in California when he visited the United States for the first time in 1981.

People have asked me the same questions that I have been asking myself all these years: Who is Babaji? What is he? Wherefrom has he come? What was the aim or purpose for which he was living and working? Is Babaji here, or has he disappeared or vanished?

So far as who is Babaji, I have not been able to get a conclusive or satisfactory answer to that. About the miracles of Baba, of course, we know of many of them. Since I first met him I have been seeing so many miracles. Even now they continue.

But the mystery that surrounds his name, that is what has been bothering me all these years. We used to see Neem Karoli Baba from very close quarters, but still he was a mystery all the time. We have seen him as a human being with a certain form and shape, but we were never sure about the form or the shape. Devotees have taken dozens of pictures. If you look at those pictures you find Babaji appearing in different forms, in different sizes, in different shapes, in different stature. Whenever any devotee asks me what was the real stature or height or weight or size of Babaji, I cannot answer. When the murti for the Kainchi ashram was to be constructed, Siddhi Didi asked me, "Dada, let us have a picture for the statue which will give a correct impression of Babaji." I could only tell her, "You shouldn't talk like that. You and I have been two of the few fortunate ones who have seen Babaji at very close quarters. Not only when he's sitting and talking, but taking his bath, going to the latrine, or taking his food or sleeping. We have never seen him of the same size or the same girth or the same height or the same weight." This has been a problem that has baffled us all throughout time.

We all know that Babaji has been a human being with human form and shape. But if we confine our attention merely to the physical, to the body, we cannot understand him. We find that even with the physique of a human being, he had the energy, he had the power, he had the love and affection that does not come to a human being. The greatest human beings of whom we read in history, no doubt they have done and achieved so many things. But what Babaji, or a saint like him, could achieve was certainly not in the capacity of the individual human being. If that is so, we must conclude that in that human body there was some force, some authority, that was not human.

From my study of the lives of the great saints or sages, who have been called incarnations of God, I have learned what they used to do, how they used to live. From this study I have come to the conclusion that Babaji was no doubt of human form, but he was actually a saint or a divine being. A saint has been defined in the *Bhagavad Gita* as a person with dual aspects—the divine and the human. From the divine aspect, Babaji had all the qualities, all the virtues, all the power and authority of a divine being. Many of us have seen various of the powers that Babaji used to wield: he could atomize himself, take the form of a fly and go out of the room or building, he could take a gigantic form as did Hanuman crossing to Lanka in the *Ramayana*, he could move about anywhere, he could know what was in our minds, what has taken place so many years back, and what is to come. These things were so very common and simple for him.

Saints or sages are realized souls, those who have freed themselves from the doctrine of karma, fate or destiny. They are no longer slaves, no more at the mercy of birth and death. They take birth out of their own free and voluntary choice. Why do the saints and sages go on taking human form and undergoing all those hardships and trials that human beings have got to undergo? It has been said that they come as a blessing to the world. They take birth in order to help, to assist, to deliver, to elevate the downtrodden, the fallen, the helpless. I believe Babaji had that purpose.

The methods of working of the different saints and sages are not the same. Some of them, some of the greatest ones, may be living in the dark caves in the Himalayas or in the forest, but even from there they are blessing mankind—their very presence goes on creating spiritual vibration, purifying the atmosphere. Other saints and sages may be living in human society. Some might be sadhus living in ashrams or mosques. Others might be wandering here and there. Some might be living as householders, never owning saffron clothes or matted locks. Babaji would talk about so many of them, each with different methods of working, but each and every one with the same aim—the showering of grace onto the people.

We do not know about Maharajji's education, or the forms of sadhana he had undergone, or what guru he had. We only know that before the ashrams at Kainchi and Vrindaban were built he was moving all the time. For how many years he had been moving like that, how many places he had visited, how many persons he had initiated or delivered from their miseries, nobody can say. We have knowledge only about particular places or times, a small fraction of his life. I have met most of his very closest and oldest devotees and all agree that we have known only a part of his life. Although the life of Babaji was quite a long one, it was only since the sixties that he stayed at the ashrams in Kainchi and Vrindaban or places like Nainital. Even at the ashrams Baba would be running away at the first opportunity. Also, he might be sitting with us, he might be talking with us, but he could also be roaming, moving about in another place or another world at the same time. There are so many cases of Babaji being seen in two or three different places at the same time. His body might be in meditation, but he might not be in it.

Babaji was essentially and fundamentally not a householder, nor an ashramite. From 1971, he starting saying so often every day, "Dada, what is attachment for a sadhu? I will run away, I will run away." He would not let us ask about this, but we knew that he had gotten completely tired, and he wanted to run away. We knew this very well.

Why then, if Babaji so loved moving about like a tramp, did he open ashrams? The time that he was in the ashram in Kainchi or Vrindaban and some small time also in Allahabad, he was giving his bhandara, giving his prasad, feeding the people. In what way is this the showering of his grace or showing his compassion and love to the people? In a country like America, you do not know what food means to the common people. You do not suffer hunger and starvation. But

in India you will find that so many are going hungry or suffering from malnutrition. Food is a very precious and a very valuable thing. The places that he chose, such as Kainchi, are surrounded by villagers who are very poor. Babaji therefore started the bhandara, the feeding, so that these people would be able to get some food. He would be talking not of the Bhagavad Gita or Upanishads or *Ramayana*. He would say, "God comes before the hungry as food. Give them food first, then talk to them of God." So one way of showering his love and showing his affection for the people was to remove their suffering in the form of hunger or starvation.

But it was not merely food he was giving. He was also trying to mitigate the sufferings or hardships of as many people as possible in other ways also. Some poor farmer would come and say, "Out of my pair of bullocks, my source of livelihood, one bullock has died and I have no money to purchase another." Another would say, "My daughter has reached a marriageable age. I have to get her married and I do not have the money for the dowry." Some other persons would be coming saying, "My relative is suffering from tuberculosis and I cannot afford to get help." Many of them would come because they couldn't pay their children's school fees. Babaji had a secret way of helping and assisting so many people, in ways he did not publicize. He may not be distributing the money himself, others would be doing that. But he may be telling somebody, "Take care of her," or "Give to him."

Perhaps the worst kind of suffering comes when a man or woman feels completely helpless—that there is nobody to stand by me, no one to whom I can look or ask for any kind of benefit. Very few of us can be so very religious or noble-minded as to feel or think that God is always with us and we need only look to him. We need some sort of tangible support near us, someone on whom we can lean, in whom we can put our faith or our trust. Babaji would be going to the houses of so many persons—helpless people living in helpless conditions—consoling them, giving words of cheer, trying to bring some smiles to them. We do not know how many tears of helpless women or children or men he has wiped out by his sweet words, by his compassionate touch.

You may say these are certainly not the functions or duties of the saints or sages, this is the duty of householders. That of course

Babaji did not accept. He said, "You must make a beginning here." But side by side with this he was also looking to our spiritual life, to our moral life, and to our religious life. Did we come for the food or the nice talk he was giving us? Did we get anything more from him, something that was actually entering our hearts and making a seat there? Was he giving us any kind of example or any kind of lesson or any kind of teaching indirectly by his gestures or by his talk, which was trying to elevate us, enoble us, teach us some of the highest virtues or the qualities of human life? Was he not actually doing that?

If Babaji is a saint, actually an ocean of love and compassion, how are we to share, how are we to enjoy that love and compassion? Can we have a claim? Can we have a right to that? People are interested in so many things—maybe cricket, maybe the cinema, maybe the sadhus or saints. We go to satisfy our passing enthusiasm and then we may forget that interest. We may be going to saints or sadhus simply to satisfy our curiosity and that ends the matter. But in the case of Babaji, like many of the saints, there have been many persons who wanted to have some sort of binding relationship—that our love, our interest in Babaji should not end. We want to have something durable, something permanent, something continuous, so that we can have a claim on him and he can also accept us and acknowledge us. We become related when a saint or sage accepts us as his or her disciple, when we take him to be our guru. Then we have that kind of permanent, beautiful relationship.

Can we say that Babaji is our guru? Can we say that he accepts us as his disciples? So far as a guru and disciple relationship is concerned, that is made when the saint or sage gives mantra or initiates someone to the divine path or light. How is the mantra given? Did Babaji give you mantra? Those of you who were with him may claim that he has given you mantra, but what about those who have not met him in his physical body, can they claim Babaji is their guru and they are also tied to him and he has got a responsibility or duty toward them?

This institution of guru and disciple is as old in India as Hinduism, as India's religious past. In most cases, there may be a guru that is going to the home of the disciple after performing some ceremonies, giving him mantra in his ear. These practices go on in so many houses, so many villages, in so many states of India. But Babaji, of course, did that only in a few cases. We find out that just giving mantra is something like sowing the seeds—there are many different methods. A small farmer with a very limited amount of land goes on sowing the seeds in individual holes. When the farm is bigger in size, the farmer scatters the seed. Where the land is vast, as in your country, you have various kinds of mechanical devices. Now think of the gardener or cultivator who goes on growing the forest or the trees over the entire universe. Think of the God or the divine being who goes on planting the seeds over the entire world. He must have some devices.

There might be some gurus, priests, who go to each and every individual and give mantra. But the greater ones have got different ways of doing it, for example, Ramakrishna Paramahansa. Sitting in Dakshineshwar, in that small ashram, he went on initiating so many thousands of people. Was he pulling everybody by the ear, taking them to a secret closed room and whispering the mantra? What about Chaitanya Mahaprabhu, that great incarnation of Krishna, going through the streets singing the name of God? In Allahabad you will find people are singing Ram bhajan or they are reading from the *Ramayana*, because Babaji used to say, "By taking the name of Ram, everything is accomplished. In this *Kali Yuga*, nobody can go for kundalini yoga; they should take the name of Ram." This was Babaji's way of scattering the seeds and giving mantra.

There are those who have not heard those things from Babaji's mouth. But it has been said that a sage or saint can give you mantra in vision or dreams. Swami Sivananda, the great saint who had so many thousands and thousands of disciples, says that if you become interested in a certain saint or sadhu—and he speaks of the great saints or great sages—if you become interested in him, if you have developed a love for him, then you can take it that he is your guru. There may be some one saint or sage who you begin loving so much, that you would not like to lose him, that you want to feel that he is your own. Now Sivananda says, "Take it that he is your guru and you can actually claim yourself to be his disciple."

There should be no difficulty in recognizing Neem Karoli Baba to be your guru, though you may or may not have met him. Even if you have met him and sat in front of him, he may not have told you, "Now look here, I am giving this mantra to you." He was

saying Ram Ram, that he was doing all the twenty-four hours, and saying that Ram Ram is the be-all and the end-all of people's lives and that by taking the name of Ram everything is accomplished. I think it all becomes so very easy and so very clear.

Another question that comes is that if Babaji is such a mighty person, such a great saint, how does he go on picking or choosing his disciples? There are millions of people in India and in your country, too. All of them have not been attracted. All of them have not gone to him, neither has he come and visited your country and been with you. Now ask yourself this question. How have you been drawn towards him?

I have seen with my own eyes that there are many persons who have been interested in seeing Babaji or meeting Babaji. They may have come to the ashram, they may have waited for him in the road, but they were never able to see him because Babaji didn't draw them, didn't want to initiate them. The old devotees in India have all seen this. We would be ten sitting and nine of us would see Babaji and the tenth would not. Or someone would be sitting on the road and Babaji would pass before him and the person wouldn't see Babaji. This happened on so many occasions. Someone would tell Babaji, "So and so is a great devotee and wants to see you." And Babaji would say, "No, I don't want to see him. He's a big badmash, I don't want to see him." So I must say that nobody would come to Babaji, nobody would know, nobody would feel interested in him, if Babaji did not want it. Babaji has actually drawn me, drawn you, that is how we are here.

When the farmer sows his seeds, he is selective about his fields, choosing those which are suitable for cultivation. If the land can be properly conditioned, then he would plant it. If the land is rocky or barren, he would not sow seeds there. The saint or sage knows that not every individual is suitable for spiritual initiation. Some might be completely ready; their past karma might be going in their favor and they can be immediately called and initiated. In the case of others, the guru would draw them near, watch over them and prepare them. I believe that no one comes to Babaji without him wanting them. We think we are running after the guru, but he is actually running after us. Why does he do it? He is not fond of your money; he is not fond of the sweet or nice things you talk about him; he is not fond of the publicity you can make about him. It is out of sheer grace, out of sheer kindness.

You must know that a sage or a saint has got the whole wealth of the world at his disposal. He has got no needs, no requirements of his own. He doesn't worry about food, clothes, money, nothing of the sort. A guru is there to carry the big loads or burdens of his disciples. This is what the guru goes on doing, giving and giving and giving to you. That giving we cannot call charity, which is a word that comes from our family references, our business life, our day-to-day life. A gift or charity is made to one from whom we have received something in the past or hope to get something in the future. When a gift is given, the relationship between the person making the gift and receiving it comes to be one superior and the other inferior. Somebody who goes on receiving charity, getting gifts, can never himself be very proud or very happy. But in the case of grace, anybody who has got the grace of God feels himself so elevated. "Oh, I have become something divine. I have been elevated." So when the grace of the guru comes, its purpose is to elevate, to raise and lift people.

Now we know that a sage or a saint does not want anything, he has no need of his own, but still, out of grace, he makes you work for him, makes you give to him. A guru comes to have a claim not only on your physical labor and exertion, but also on the working of your mind and on every possession. Tan-man-dhan [body-mind-wealth]. Your guru can claim it all.

In India, when you go to a temple and the priest performs a puja or any kind of prayer or ceremony, you must pay him a fee. You might also give prasad, rich clothes and ornaments to the deity, but if you don't pay the priest, your worship is not complete. Similarly, a guru is taking a lump of clay and turning it into something permanent and beautiful and abiding. When he is transforming you from a lump of clay into something precious, he must take a fee from you, otherwise your spiritual growth and journey would not be complete. If the guru does not accept the fee from us, all our efforts will be absolutely useless.

Sometimes the guru has got to be cruel, has got to punish us, simply because willingly, voluntarily, we would not be able to give away our valuable or precious things. The guru says we have got to make the journey, we have got to reach the goal.

It has been said that there are three main functions of the guru. The first is the work of the swan. The swan is one of the creatures that can separate milk from water. If you or I mix milk and water together, we cannot then separate them. Similarly, if sugar and sand are mixed, we cannot separate them, but the ant can. So the swan, called the hans, can differentiate the real from the unreal, the useful from the useless. Ramakrishna was called Paramahans, which means the great swan, because he could take from this jungle of worldly life what is real, precious and valuable, the crest jewel, from the superficial and useless. You and I cannot know what is the actual path of bliss, what is the road for the divine life. So a guru first of all goes on showing the disciples what is real, what is unreal, what is precious, what is worthless, which is the road you must walk, which you must discard.

In America, when your ironware or tools become rusted and useless, you throw them out. But in India there is a class of blacksmith who collects this scrap iron which is no longer suitable for any kind of work. They go on removing the dross or rust, the external elements, from the pure iron that may be there. This is also the second thing the guru does whenever a new disciple is chosen. He takes the rusted iron and puts it through hard treatment. The greater the dross, the hotter the fire the guru must use to reclaim the pure iron, to make it useful and valuable, to make it serve the purpose that is still there. The great gurus can reclaim us, no matter how very rotten or useless we may have become.

Those of you who have been in India know that, in place of plastics or glassware, clay pots are used as utensils. In each and every village there are potters who collect the clay, make it into a paste, and then try to bring a form or shape to it. Each utensil has got to be completely smooth, without any edge, without any leakage. When they put the clay on the wheel to shape it, two things are necessary. First there must be some force or pressure used to shape the clay. Yet if the clay is unprotected or unguarded, the pressure would break the pot. So what the potter does is use one hand to go on beating the clay into a shape, but the other hand is kept inside the pot, saving it and protecting it from the outward force or pressure. This is the third thing the guru does.

You have read the life of Milarepa. His guru Marpa was outwardly so very cruel and hard that even his wife was complaining, "Why do you do this?" But look at his inner heart, how very affectionate, how very soft, how very gentle, how very gracious the guru was in order to protect his disciple. So we find that the guru is compassion. But if merely compassion or softness takes form, not bringing any pressure, not applying any force, then the pot would not be made. So in our heart of hearts we should feel that when Babaji has drawn us to him, it is not merely a joke, you see that. If he has drawn us, he must certainly be interested in our welfare. He wants us to be worthy of something. If we have this faith or trust in the guru, then that would be the most valuable, the most precious thing for our spiritual journey, for our future growth and development.

ॐ ॐ

XV
EPILOGUE

I visited his ashrams for a couple of years after Babaji took his samadhi. It was during these visits that I realized I was not fitting in well under the new environment. Sometimes I could not decide what was to be done. Then I was reminded of what he had said in 1962, "Dada, you stay at home." I did not understand then why he wanted me to do so. The understanding came when my excursions to his ashrams proved to be a failure.

After I had stopped visiting the ashrams, some ardent devotees started saying, "Dada has left Baba." When faced with a statement like this, the only reply I could give was, "When did I catch hold of Baba that I could leave him now? He caught me! I could never catch him, so there is no question of leaving him." That is all of it.

राम राम

In Honored and Loving Memory

Sudhir "Dada" Mukerjee

November 26, 1913 – September 10, 1997

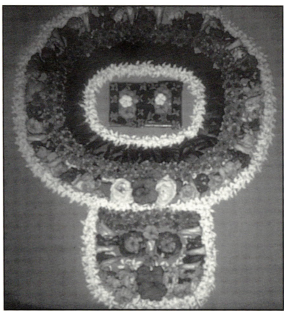

Below, one of Dada's daily floral offerings on Maharajji's tucket; above, one of Didi's watercolors of these pujas.

GLOSSARY

accha (p. 84) a much used Hindi word of imprecise meaning, variously: good, yes?, oh?, ah so!
amrit (p. 19) nectar
Ardha Mela (p. 18) mela held on the sixth year between Khumba Melas
arti (p. 105) ceremony of light, Hindu ritual for honoring deities
ashirbad (p. 60) blessing
ashram (p. 3) hermitage, monastery
baba, babaji (pp. 4, 1) title for an elder or holy man. The suffix "ji" is frequently added to a name as an indication of respect
badmash (p. 45) rascal, troublemaker
Bhagavad Gita (p. 172) a celebrated Hindu mystical poem
bhajan (p. 79) devotional song
bhandara (p. 22) feast
brahmin (p. 3) priest class in Hindu caste system
chai (p. 39) sweet tea
chapati (p. 34) unleavened flatbread
chaukidar (p. 39) gatekeeper or doorkeeper
Chitrakut (p. 39) forest area south of Allahabad where, in the *Ramayana*, Ram, Sita, and Lakshman spent 13 years after being banished from Ayodhya. Now a place of pilgrimage
dacoit (p. 83) bandit, robber
Dakshineshwar (p. 2) location of Ramakrishna Paramahansa's ashram outside of Calcutta
dal (p. 62) lentils, which can be of several varieties: mung, chana, araharki, etc.
dandi (p. 40) litter, palanquin
darshan (p. 8) spiritual audience
devi (p. 85) goddess
dharma (p. 105) spiritual way of life
dharmashala (p. 80) hostel, especially for pilgrims
dhoti (p. 3) cloth used to cover lower part of a man's body
dhuni (p. 141) campfire, especially that of a sadhu
Durga (p. 85) aspect of the Divine Mother

ganja (p. 35) marijuana
Gayatri (p. 3) aspect of the Divine Mother
ghat (p. 41) steps and platform beside a river, used for bathing or cremation
ghee (p. 69) clarified butter
guru (p. 1) spiritual teacher
Guru Purnima (p. 135) holiday in July for honoring the guru
halva (p. 95) sweet made of wheat, ghee, and sugar
Hanuman, Hanumanji (p. 31) son of the wind, the monkey god, perfect servant of Rama
Hanuman Chaleesa (p. 93) hymn of forty verses in honor of Hanuman
havan (p. 69) sacrificial fire ceremony
Holi (p. 88) Hindu holiday commemorating the play of Krishna and the gopis
jaleebi (p. 89) fried Indian sweet in sugar syrup
jata (p. 70) long, matted hair piled on the head, usually worn by sadhus
Kali (p. 85) terrifying aspect of the Divine Mother
Kali Yuga (p. 177) the age of darkness
khir (p. 43) a rice pudding
kirtan (p. 21) group singing of devotional songs
Krishna (p. 3) an incarnation of the god Vishnu
Kumbha Mela (p. 20) a great spiritual gathering held every twelve years in Allahabad or Hardwar
laddu (p. 97) sweet favored by Hanuman
lakh (p. 78) one hundred thousand
Lakshmi (p. 63) goddess of good fortune
Lakshmi-Narayana (p. 85) Narayana is an aspect of the god Vishnu and Lakshmi is his consort
langoti (p. 155) loin cloth
lila (p. 21) play
lingam (p. 3) phallic symbol of the god Shiva
lota (p. 20) water pot
Magh Mela (p. 35) spiritual gathering held every six years
Maharajji (p. 7) great king, frequent form of address for sadhus and holy men
mahasamadhi (p. 147) great samadhi, i.e., final samadhi of a realized being
mandir (p. 31) temple
mantra (p. 1) devotional incantation to an aspect of God
maya (p. 61) illusion
murti (p. 31) consecrated statue
Naga baba (p. 127) naked sadhu

GLOSSARY 189

Narmadeshwar (p. 58) special polished stones from the Narmada River, believed to be meteorites
panchamrita (p. 135) literally, five nectars; a mixture of ghee, yogurt, honey, milk and rose water used in religious ceremonies
pranam (p. 149) to bow down to
prasad (p. 7) consecrated food
puja (p. 3) prayer ritual
pujari (p. 31) temple priest
puri (p. 69) fried flat bread
Rama (p. 3) an incarnation of the god Vishnu
Ramayana (p. 83) story of Rama's life
Ras Lila (p. 18) staged presentation of the story of Krishna and the gopis (milkmaids)
rishi (p. 71) sage, especially one who lived before the present era
rudhraksha (p. 70) seed used to make prayer beads
rupee (p. 40) Indian "dollar"
sacred thread ceremony (p. 1) initiation ceremony of brahmin boys
sadhana (p. 75) spiritual practice
sadhu (p. 3) renunciate
samadhi (p. 147) spiritual trance
sangam (p. 20) confluence of sacred rivers
sari (p. 51) draped garment worn by Hindu women
satsang (p. 32) spiritual group or gathering
Shiva (p. 3) the destructive aspect of God
siddhi (p. 164) spiritual power
Sombari Maharaj (p. 71) famous saint of the Kumoan hill area, who died many years ago
Sundarakand (p. 90) chapter of the *Ramayana* which relates the exploits of Hanuman in Lanka
tapasya (p. 71) austerities
tiffin (p. 55) lunch, or container for carrying lunch
tucket (p. 91) wooden bed
Upanishads (p. 130) a collection of Hindu esoteric texts
Vaishnava (p. 35) sect devoted to the god Vishnu
Vibishan (p. 83) character in the *Ramayana*, who becomes a friend of Hanuman
Vindhyavasini Devi (p. 43) a famous murti of the Goddess in the Vindhya hills area
wallah (p. 39) vendor, proprietor
yagna (p. 69) major sacrificial fire ceremony